IMAGES
of America

FLORAL CITY

IMAGES
of America

FLORAL CITY

Tom Ritchie, Frank Peters,
and Paulette Lash Ritchie

ARCADIA
PUBLISHING

Copyright © 2012 by Tom Ritchie, Frank Peters, and Paulette Lash Ritchie ISBN 978-1-5316-6350-6

Published by Arcadia Publishing
Charleston, South Carolina

Library of Congress Control Number: 2011945827

For all general information, please contact Arcadia Publishing: Telephone 843-853-2070
Fax 843-853-0044
E-mail sales@arcadiapublishing.com
For customer service and orders:
Toll-Free 1-888-313-2665

Visit us on the Internet at www.arcadiapublishing.com

This book is dedicated to the pioneering families of Floral City who endured through the years and made the town what it is today. We owe a great debt of gratitude to those who came before us, and we value the contributions they made to leave us with such a wonderful community.

CONTENTS

ACKNOWLEDGMENTS

All the photographs herein are from the Citrus County Historical Society, Inc., collection, unless otherwise noted. Sincere gratitude is given to those who have donated these wonderful images to the historical society and its local branch, the Floral City Heritage Council. We appreciate their generosity for allowing us to use these photographs in this book.

We are also indebted to the Florida State Archives and the US Geological Survey Photographic Library, both of which made their collections of historical photographs available to us.

Special thanks are given to Florida artist Jackson Walker for allowing us to use an image of his magnificent painting *The Macon Greys*, which depicts a historic moment at Fort Cooper during the Second Seminole War. The painting is now in the collection of the US Army National Guard Bureau.

The Citrus County Historical Society has been very generous to allow us to donate all the author's proceeds from this book to its subsidiary, the Floral City Heritage Council.

INTRODUCTION

Floral City is one of the oldest communities in Citrus County and retains the old-time ambiance of a sleepy southern town. It is an attractive community with a lot of pleasing, old-style architecture that has survived from the late 19th and early 20th centuries. The majestic live oaks shading the houses and streets give the place a feel of age and tranquility. The story of Floral City begins long before the town was established, and the fascinating history of the site fits into the bigger sequence of events that shaped Florida. When studying the town's past, it is important to take into account its early development because the area has been appreciated by humans for millennia.

Native people inhabited the site of Floral City for countless generations before Europeans arrived. Pre-Columbian Indians of the Timucuan cultural group lived here from as early as 800 AD in a village called Tocaste until it was abandoned in the 1540s. Its demise was brought about by the arrival of the first Europeans, Spanish conquistadors who explored the area in search of gold and glory but left behind disease, death, and destruction.

Two major Spanish expeditions visited the site of Floral City in the early 16th century. The first was a disastrous expedition led by Panfilo de Narváez, who was awarded settlement rights to Florida in 1527 by King Charles I. De Narváez arrived in central Florida with about 450 men and made an extended stop at Tocaste. His chronicler, Alvar Nuñez Cabeza de Vaca, one of only four survivors, later described Tocaste in the fascinating account of his adventures, a book titled *La Relacion*, which he produced in Mexico City, making it the first real American book.

The other Spanish expedition to visit Tocaste was led by Hernando de Soto in 1539. His large company of more than 500 men brought horse, mules, and a herd of 260 pigs. The pigs that escaped gave rise to the wild hogs found in central Florida today. De Soto's chronicler, Inca Garcilasso de la Vega, gave glowing descriptions of the territory and Indian way of life, but de Soto was ruthless and violent, and his behavior soured the Southeastern Indians against all Europeans for years to come. European diseases, the slave trade, and war between Spain and England essentially depopulated Florida by the beginning of the 18th century.

Creek Indians moved in to fill the void, and the site of Floral City was resettled in the 1760s, when Seminole Indians established a village here named Cho-illy-hadjo. Scottish farmers and traders settled nearby in 1776 during the Revolutionary War because Florida remained loyal to the British crown. The first American settlers moved into the area immediately after Florida became a US territory in 1821. Cho-illy-hadjo village was destroyed by American soldiers in 1836 during the Second Seminole War. Its location and destruction were recorded by an observant US soldier, Lt. Henry Prince, who left a diary that was eventually published as *Amidst a Storm of Bullets*. The Seminoles were driven out of the area by 1842, at which time many more settlers began homesteading in the Floral City region.

Over thousands of years, numerous pre-Columbian cultural groups, including Ice Age nomads, pre-Ceramic hunter-gatherers, and village-based agriculturists, as well as Spaniards, Britons, and Americans have all coveted this area abundant in fresh water, rich soil, a mild climate, vast forests, and plentiful fish and game. It is fortunate that several early historical accounts have given us insight into the people and events in the proximity of Floral City long before the town officially came into being in 1883.

In 1884, photographer C.B. Colby was hired to promote Floral City through a series of 25 pictures of the new town and its environs. The following advertisement was printed on the back of each stereoscopic photograph card:

> FLORAL CITY, a newly laid out town, is located on a high elevation on a peninsula between Chalo (Tsala) Apopka Lake and Lake Consuela, nestling among the hills, its sandy beach skirted with mammoth live oaks. Chalo Apopka Lake is eighteen miles long and has a lake shore of seventy-five miles; it is situated in the great orange belt, in a climate entirely free from damaging frosts, where all kinds of vegetation and semi-tropical fruits flourish to perfection. The hotel at Floral City, seventy feet above the lake, gives excellent fare to all who wish to visit the Venice of the lakes in the Italy of America. There is no place in Florida where the sportsman can gratify his taste more fully than here. The lake is full of fish, while the woods are teeming with deer, turkey, and small game of all kinds.

From its humble beginnings, the town has gone through boom and bust. Floral City experienced a major transformation at the end of the 1800s with the coming of the railroad, when the town's commercial center was moved more than half a mile away from its lakeshore origins to its present location. An economic shift from citrus production to phosphate mining occurred in the early 1900s, and the population quickly grew to about 10,000 people, making it the largest town in Citrus County. For a time, Floral City had a "wild west" feel with rowdy cowboys, saloons, shootings, posses, claim jumping, and land speculation.

By and large, however, Floral City was a peaceful and modern town. Residents enjoyed the telegraph, electricity, and telephone service earlier than most because Floral City was the base of operations for several phosphate mining companies. Soon after the beginning of World War I, the town suffered a severe economic depression, followed by a great fire, and it reverted back to its original state: a small, laid-back, southern community.

Floral City is an old town by Florida standards, but while many contemporary communities in west central Florida have long since disappeared, this town has endured. The National Register of Historic Places has listed an official Floral City Historic District, which includes portions of the residential area on both sides of the main street, Orange Avenue, the trees all along Aroostook Way, and the Puckett property on Levy Lane as well as several commercial buildings and the Methodist church.

One

THE EARLY DAYS

All these pre-Colombian projectile points were found near Floral City. Their time frame spans nearly 9,000 years. Each point's name and associated cultural period are cataloged here, from left to right, as follows: Santa Fe, Late Paleo-Indian (9000–8000 BC); Bolen plain, Early Dalton (8000–7000 BC); Arredondo, Early Pre-Ceramic Archaic (6000–5000 BC); Marion, Middle Pre-Ceramic Archaic (5000–3000 BC); Clay, Culbreath, and Lafayette, all from the Late Pre-Ceramic Archaic (3000–2000 BC); and Citrus, Florida Transitional (1200–500 BC).

The first Europeans to explore Florida encountered people of the Safety Harbor culture, part of the Timucuan linguistic group. These Native Americans were described as being very tall and muscular, often adorned with spectacular tattoos. Jacques le Moyne chronicled life among the Florida aborigines in 1564 and 1565 with 42 drawings and an accompanying written narrative.

The Timucuans were hunters and depended primarily on white-tailed deer for survival, utilizing this stealthy strategy to approach prey, which impressed Le Moyne. They were also agriculturists, growing maize, squash, and beans, and fishers, using nets and ropes woven from plant fibers to catch fish for consumption and trade in the Withlacoochee River and local lakes.

By 700 AD, the Indian village Tocaste existed at the present site of Floral City. It was located along the southern shore of Lake Tsala Apopka and was inhabited until the mid-1500s. In 1528, Spanish conquistadors noted round pole-and-thatch houses and that the Indians depended on dugout canoes made from bald cypress or pine logs.

Two Spanish expeditions visited Tocaste in the early 1500s. Panfilo de Narváez came in 1528. In 1539, Hernando de Soto, shown here, stayed three days, threatening the Indians and demanding food and information about gold. The Spaniards confiscated the Indians' critical winter food stores when they departed, which led to deadly conflict when the Indians ambushed them a few miles away.

Early European explorers sometimes described Florida as the Garden of Eden. They were impressed by the Indian way of life and admired the beautiful, comfortable environment in which they lived. De Soto's chronicler, Inca Garcilasso de la Vega, described west central Florida as "a wilderness, filled with oak trees, pines and trees unknown in Spain, but arranged in equal distances that they seem planted for pleasure." This 19th-century engraving by Granville Perkins depicts de Soto's bivouac a few days after they set off on their four-year expedition from Tampa Bay, which would put them near Tocaste, on the present site of Floral City. This idyllic scene belies the coming conflict between the two races, including the introduction of deadly European diseases that ultimately led to a collapse in the aboriginal population throughout the New World and the quick abandonment of Tocaste.

The Second Seminole War, from December 1835 to December 1842, was the longest, deadliest, and most expensive of all the Indian wars fought by the US military. The first year of fighting occurred within a 20-mile radius of Floral City because the main Seminole stronghold at that time was within the nearby Cove of the Withlacoochee. These early hostilities included the inaugural Dade Battle on December 23, 1835, the First Battle of the Withlacoochee on December 31, 1835, the Second Battle of the Withlacoochee from February 27 to March 6, 1836, Scott's Invasion of the Cove of the Withlacoochee in March and April 1836, Call's Invasion of the Cove of the Withlacoochee in October 1836, and the Battle of Wahoo Swamp from November 17 to 21, 1836. During General Scott's maneuvers of 1836, a pine log breastworks named Fort Cooper was built three miles north of modern-day Floral City to house 104 soldiers under the command of Maj. Mark Cooper for 16 days while the rest of the army unsuccessfully pursued the main band of Seminole warriors. Jackson Walker's accurate painting *The Macon Greys* depicts a skirmish during a Seminole siege of Fort Cooper. (Courtesy of Jackson Walker.)

This small clay pot, found in the Floral City area, is a very rare example of Seminole pottery dating from the 1830s. By this time, the Seminoles had long since switched to superior and more durable trade items, such as iron pots, which were easily procured from white traders. However, during the Second Seminole War, when access to white trade items was cut off, they were forced to revert to traditional fire-hardened pottery. This pot was made from local clay probably found along the banks of the Withlacoochee River and would have been used to hold liquid or small amounts of dry goods, such as grain. It is part of the collection of the Floral City Heritage Museum.

Lt. Henry Prince, a career soldier from Maine who served in Florida during the Second Seminole War, kept a journal that described in detail the daily life and events that he experienced from early 1836 through mid-1838. Lieutenant Prince's diary helped archeologists find the long-sought site of Osceola's wartime settlement in the Cove of the Withlacoochee, a few miles northeast of Floral City.

Osceola was an important Indian leader during the early years of the Second Seminole War, which raged throughout Florida from 1835 to 1842. The Floral City region was the main stronghold of the Seminoles, and many battles occurred in the area. Osceola, shown here in a painting by George Catlin, was captured under a flag of truce in 1837 and died the following year.

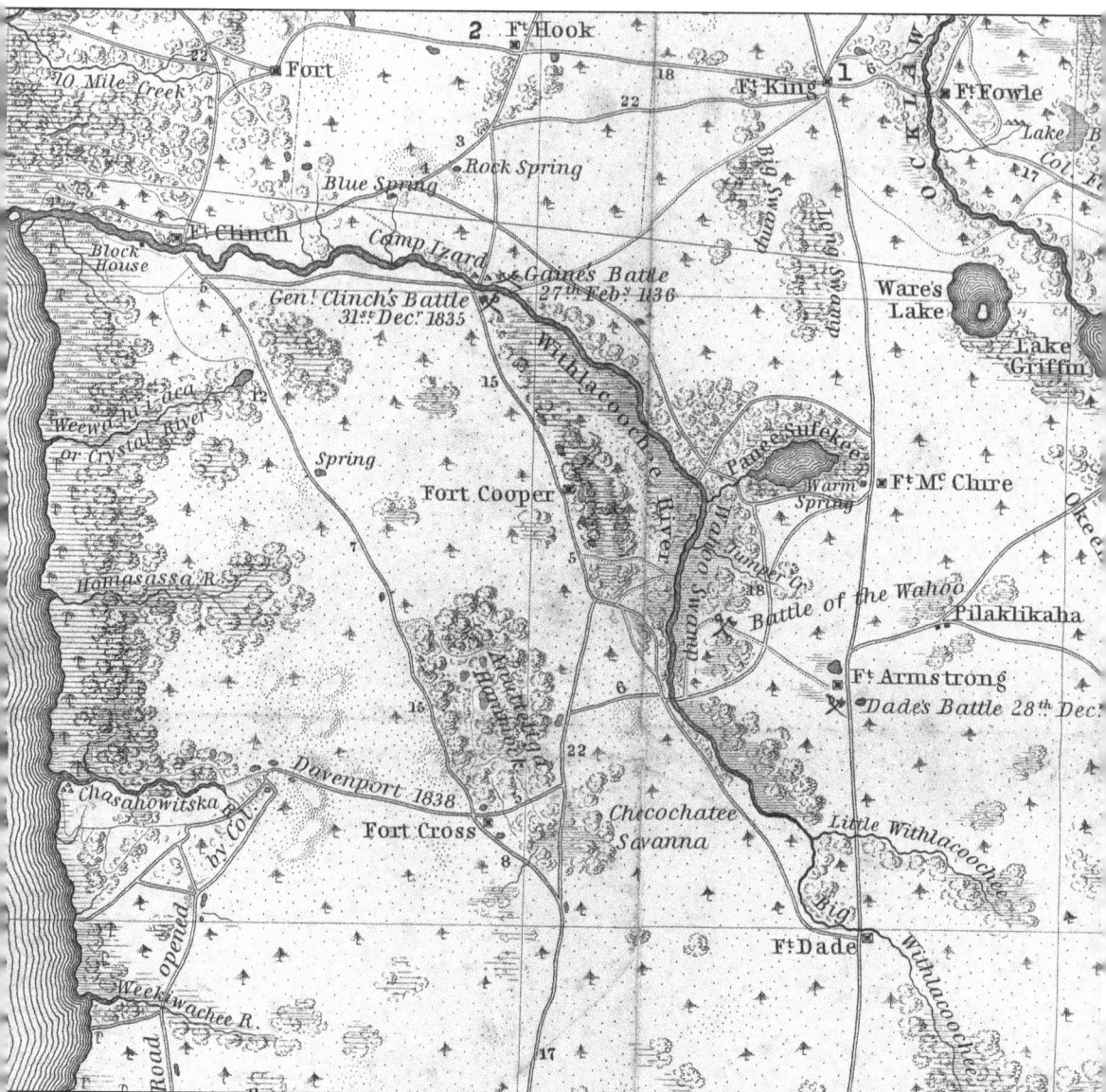

By 1839, the year this Seat of War military map was produced, seven forts had been constructed within the watershed of the Withlacoochee River. Their purpose was to give logistical support to US government forces fighting the Seminoles. The forts were strategically placed about one day's march apart. Fort Cooper was located just north of the site where Floral City would develop 44 years later. Fort Cross was located south-southwest of Floral City near the edge of the Withlacoochee State Forest. Fort Armstrong was located at the Dade battlefield about 10 miles east of Floral City, near modern-day Bushnell. Fort Clinch was 10 miles upstream from the mouth of the Withlacoochee River. Fort Izzard was a major camp near what is now Dunnellon. Fort McClure stood on the eastern shore of Lake Panasoffkee. Fort Dade overlooked the banks of the Big Withlacoochee River about six miles upstream from the confluence of the Big and Little Withlacoochee Rivers. As a point of reference, Fort King, located at the top of the map, is now Ocala.

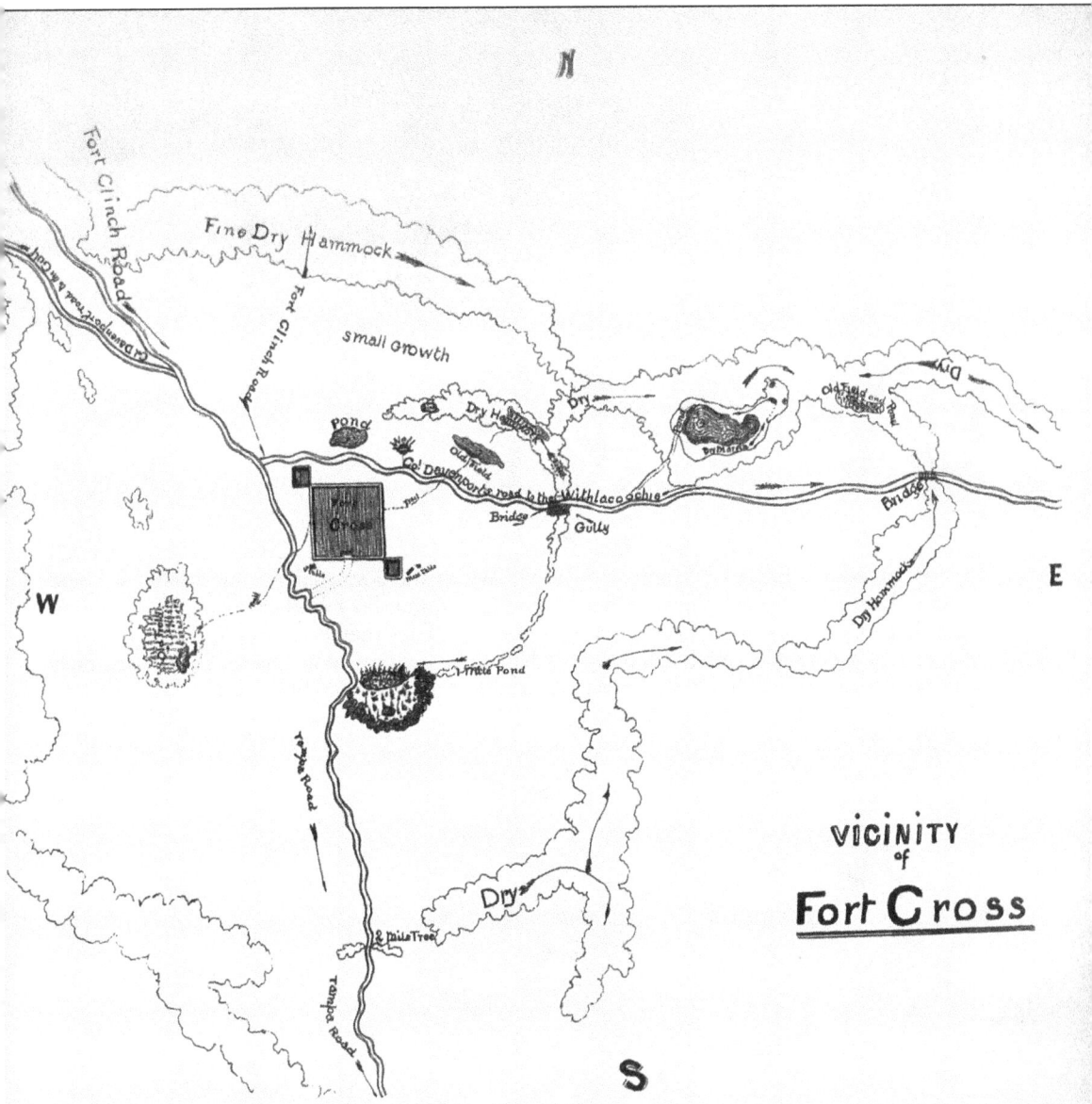

A primitive network of military trails already existed in Florida's interior by the time the Second Seminole War started, and much effort was made by US forces to quickly upgrade them and construct new ones to allow easier movement of men and equipment. Forts located along these trails were essential for the protection of the military personnel. Fort Cross, shown here in Lieutenant Prince's 1836 map, was typical of the log-based defensive fortifications used by the US military at this time. It was located at the edge of the Anutteliga Hammock, about eight miles south-southwest of Floral City near the edge of the Withlacoochee Forest. The trails shown on the map eventually grew into the present-day road system; the vertical trails became County Road 491, and the horizontal trail became County Road 480 (Stagecoach Road).

In 1863, a total of 250 federal troops landed near Bayport and destroyed the customs house, some thatched huts, several boats, numerous barrels of molasses, and about 200 bales of cotton, including some that were produced by Floral City area pioneers. They marched 12 miles to Brooksville, where they encountered and defeated a small detachment of the Home Guard. This photograph was taken during the 2001 annual January reenactment of the Brooksville raid.

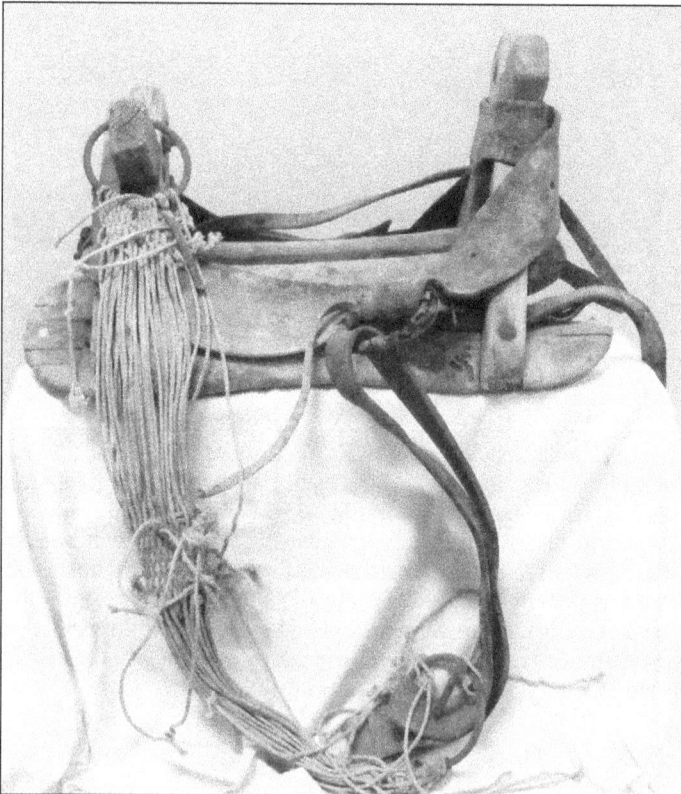

This Civil War–era packsaddle belonged to E.A. Zellner, a Confederate soldier who homesteaded a few miles east of Floral City, in Cove Bend, in the 1870s. Like many Confederate soldiers, Zellner provided some of his own supplies. The wooden saddle was used like a regular saddle, but it had four extra projections on which to hang supplies. A thick blanket was necessary to protect the animal from painful chafing.

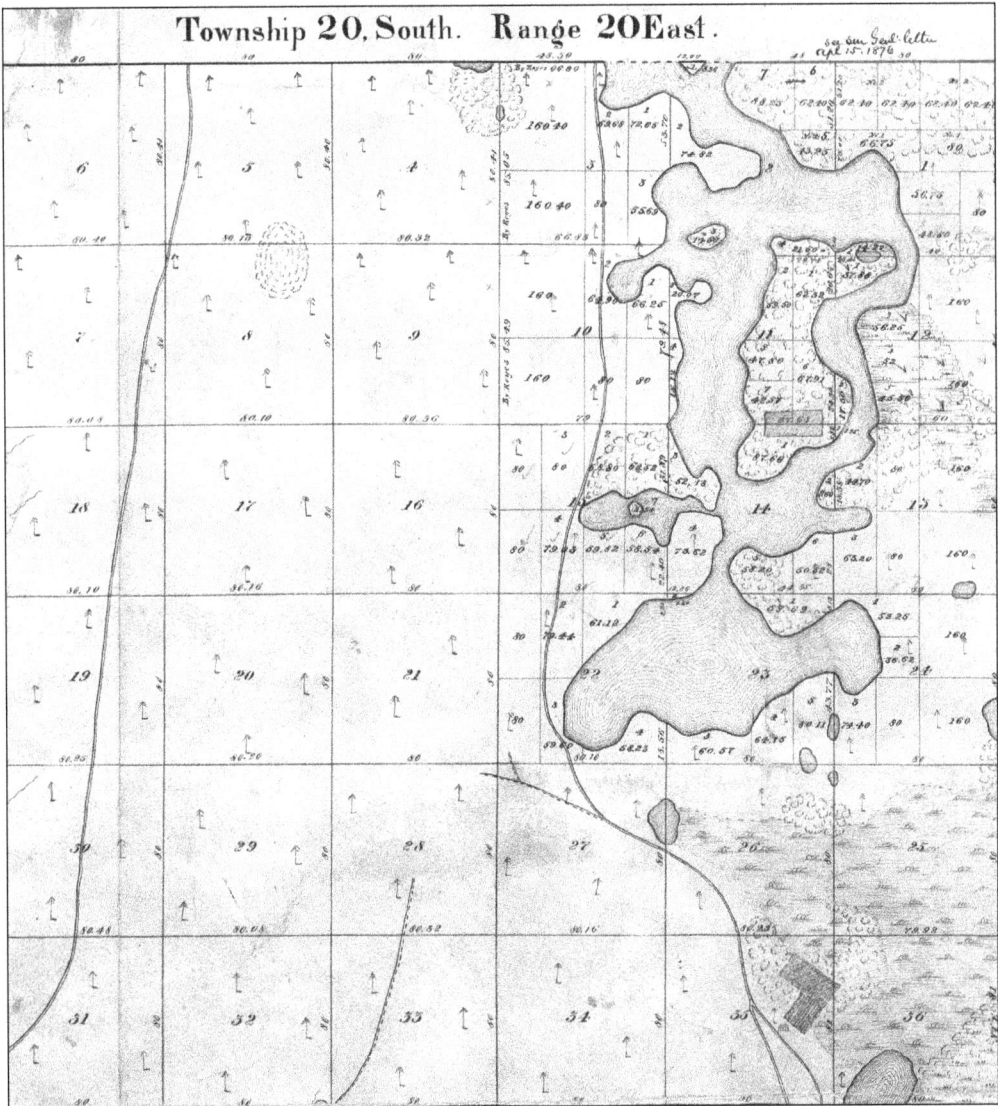

Township 20, South. Range 20 East.

This township survey map was made in 1854, nearly 30 years before Floral City was platted. The geography has not changed significantly and important landmarks are identifiable. The large southern lake section is Lake Bradley, and the small extension to the west is Lake Consuela. The main water body is the Floral City Pool and within it is Duval Island. The three military roads still exist. The one that skirts the lake system is Istachatta Road (County Road 39) coming from the south, becoming Great Oaks Drive as it passes Lakes Bradley and Consuela, and running into Old Floral City Road past Lake Tsala Apopka. The partial trail in the south-central position is part of Stagecoach Road (County Road 480) and the western one is Pleasant Grove Road (County Road 581). The rectangular cultivated field on Duval Island belonged to John Paul Formy-Duval, but the large angular cultivated land in the southeastern section is unidentified.

This two-story Classic Revival home is the oldest remaining 19th-century structure in the area, and it may be the oldest continuously occupied home in Citrus County. It is located on the southeast corner of Old Floral City Road and Orange Avenue, right next to the Floral City Heritage Hall museum. The house was built by John Paul Formy-Duval about the time of the Civil War, well before Floral City was founded. Although this house has undergone extensive modifications over the years, it is still historically significant to the local heritage and is a central part of the historic district. The southern end view (left), taken in the 1950s, clearly shows the rounded top of the old cistern on the right, under the trees.

Two

THE TOWN

In 1883, W.H. Havron (right), a surveyor and property owner in Floral City, joined forces with state senator Austin Mann, whose district included Hernando County, to develop the town. They hired Ocala photographer C.B. Colby to produce 25 stereoscopic photograph cards the following year to promote the town and its environs. These stereoviews are extremely rare, but a few have been found.

From the 1884 C.B. Colby series of stereoview cards promoting Floral City, this image looks down Aroostook Way in the newly developed town center looking north towards the Floral City Pool of Lake Tsala Apopka. The photograph was taken from the second floor of the New England Hotel. Numerous tree stumps left from clearing the road to the shoreline are still visible. It is hard to believe that this area was the original commercial center of the town, but after the construction of a steamboat pier at the end of the road, buildings soon sprang up along both sides of the road. Live oak saplings were planted to line the roadsides soon after this photograph was taken. Note the newly constructed store with the false front and corral on the right. About 10 years later, the town center, including many of the actual buildings, was moved a half-mile west to focus on the South Florida Railroad, and this area was nearly abandoned.

22

To people from the temperate regions of the north, nothing signifies a tropical paradise better than a palm tree and white sand. This C.B. Colby photograph of a cabbage palm was supposed to entice Northerners to the budding southern town. Of course, this is no tropical coconut palm, but instead a hardy plant adapted to extended freezes and periodical floods. And the sand is nowhere near an ocean beach.

This cypress swamp from the C.B. Colby series shows the beautiful, unspoiled waters in the Floral City area. The scene was meant to portray a wild and exotic look, an untamed wilderness for keen sportsmen. The photograph, labeled Cypress Pool, shows two young men perched on a log next to a crude wooden fence in what is probably a temporary flooded backwater.

This 1886 photograph of the New England Hotel shows four of the recently planted live oak saplings lined up along the barely discernible, sand-packed Orange Avenue. They are protected within wooden enclosures. Note the two tall pine tree trunks visible in the center, which were later replaced with live oaks. Unfortunately, the hotel no longer exists.

About 80 years later, the live oaks were huge, spreading trees draped with Spanish moss, seen in this 1950s photograph. This section of Orange Avenue is unquestionably one of Florida's most photographed roads. These oaks and countless others scattered around the residential area give Floral City its graceful, sleepy ambiance. Residents continually replace lost oaks to insure the canopy will endure for generations to come.

In 1887, a petition was made to the state legislature to divide Hernando County into smaller units. State senator Mann, whose district included Hernando County, strongly supported a bill that subdivided it into Hernando, Pasco, and Citrus Counties. Most people agreed with the idea of subdividing the large county, but there was contention as to where to draw the new boundaries. The county line dividing Citrus and Hernando Counties today includes a rather curious southerly extension in the southeastern corner. This was the result of Mann's influence in the process, as this compromise allowed him to include all of his vast landholdings within Citrus County. He had big plans for the ensuing growth of Citrus County, but a political setback several years later caused him to sell off his holdings and move out of the area.

The above photograph shows the new town center around 1900, a half-mile west of its original 1883 location on the shore of Lake Tsala Apopka. It was now connected to the South Florida Railroad and depot, which helped the town develop during the phosphate boom. The new business district was composed of the depot, the post office, a bottling plant, a school, a bank, a pharmacy, several dry goods and grocery stores, four churches, a livery stable, at least two barbershops, numerous boardinghouses and hotels, several restaurants and saloons, a blacksmith shop, and a sawmill. Floral City grew to be the largest town in Citrus County by 1900. Below is the town center in 1913, at its height during the phosphate boom. Both views face east on Orange Avenue. The buildings are all gone except for the twin-gabled Commercial Hotel in the distance to the left.

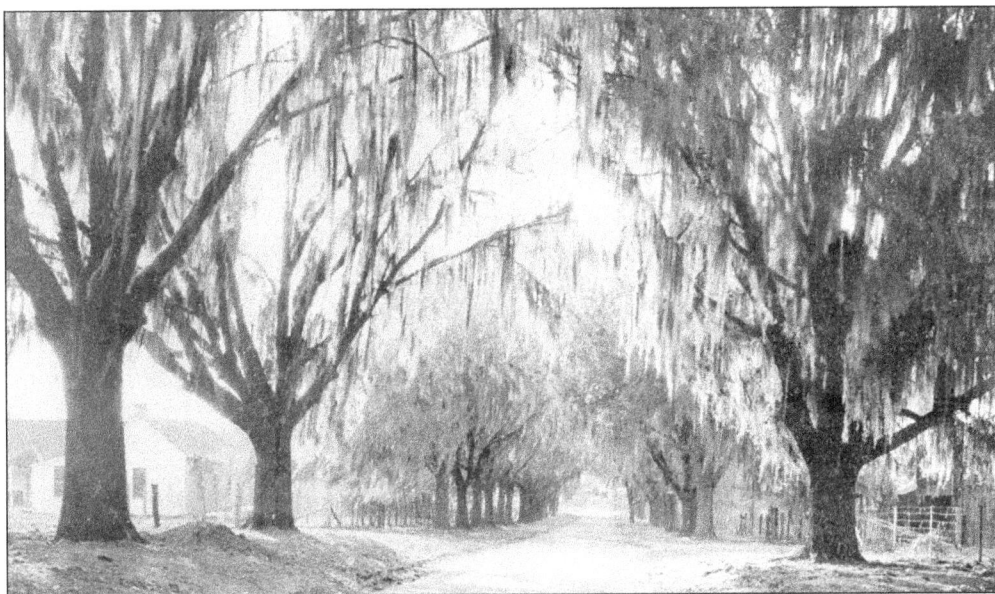

State senator Austin S. Mann and surveyor W.H. Havron named their new town after the plentiful wildflowers in the area. Members of the young community planted live oak saplings along Orange Avenue the following year. This west-facing view shows the tunnel of oaks in the 1930s, when they were 50 years old. The historic white Tanky House, still standing, is on the left.

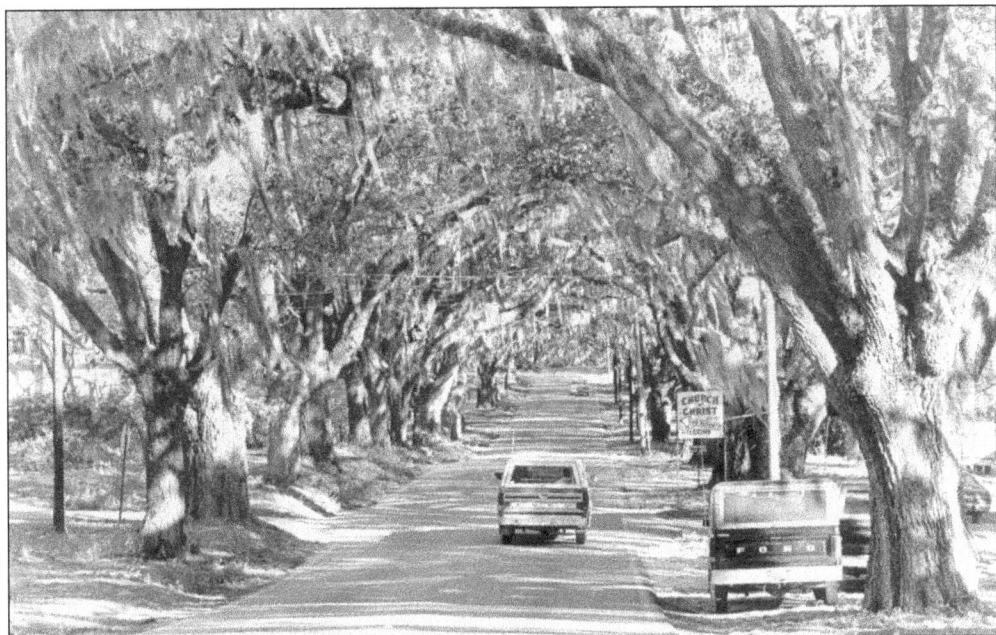

This 1981 photograph shows the tunnel of oaks looking eastward over the same stretch of Orange Avenue. The trees received a lot of care from the town's early inhabitants to help them grow so large in a century. Today, a professional arborist helps Floral City look after the trees.

Several impressive live oaks still line the residential side of Route 41 near the intersection with Orange Avenue. They provide a delightful bit of shade for motorists waiting for the stoplight to change. The historic Bellot and Smoak houses are behind the trees.

Live oak trees were also planted along several other roadways in the fledgling community. Aroostook Way was lined with live oaks at the same time as Orange Avenue, as it was then the main roadway for the commercial town center located near the steamboat pier. After the commercial center was moved to the railroad line, much of Aroostook Way became abandoned, as seen here in the 1950s.

This early-1920s aerial view of Floral City shows the watery environment so important to the history and well-being of the town. Lake Tsala Apopka fills much of the upper part of the photograph, and Lake Consuela is in the lower center. Duval Island is in the upper right. The Orange State Canal, which leads to the right from the Duval Island Bridge, is not discernible in this photograph because the water level is very high. It connects the lake system to the Withlacoochee River 2.5 miles to the east. The north-south railroad and Route 41 both cut across the lower left of the photograph, as does Orange Avenue, intersecting with Bedford Road west of the town. The tunnel of oaks lining Orange Avenue forms the diagonal dark straight line through the center of the photograph.

John Paul Formy-Duval sold off his town holdings and built a second home on Duval Island. This second house, constructed c. 1870, was very similar to the original one still standing in Floral City. It was blown off its foundation during a storm around 1900 but was still lived in for several years before it was abandoned and dismantled.

This late-1800s photograph shows Duval Island when new settlers came. Most of the forest was removed to establish citrus groves, but shade trees were left around homesites. The perimeter road was simply wheel ruts in the sandy soil. The location of this photograph is unknown, but one can see new residential fencing on the left and animal enclosure fencing on the right.

The town owes much of its character to George Higgins, a master builder who came to Floral City in the late 1800s. In addition to building some of the most important historic houses in Floral City, he also constructed two area churches, including the United Methodist Church of Floral City, in 1884. It is a splendid example of a Gothic Vernacular wood-frame church and still stands today.

George W. Higgins built this beautiful folk-Victorian house in the 1890s as his personal home. On Orange Avenue, east of Old Floral City Road, it was a showcase for his impressive contracting talents. Higgins later sold it to W.C. Zimmerman, the first clerk of the court in Citrus County. Recent owners have managed to maintain its original condition, apart from a few modern conveniences.

After selling his first Floral City home, George W. Higgins built another magnificent one in 1903. Higgins and his family lived here for many years while he continued to make a major impact on the architectural style of Floral City. It was typical of this period to formally pose family members around the house. The house was later sold to the Griner family, who made many major modifications that have changed its appearance considerably, as seen in the below photograph. It is renowned locally for its beautiful gardens and trees.

This Victorian house, with its two dominant front-facing gables, was built by a Mr. Dawsey in the late 1890s. It was owned by David Alonzo Tooke, who lived here with his family for several years before he moved out to Duval Island to raise citrus. The decorative iron fence along the front of this property was part of the fencing originally surrounding the old courthouse in Inverness.

Almost identical to the D.A. Tooke house next door, Dawsey built this structure for James Thaddeus Love. It shares the unusually high hip roof with intersecting twin gables and very tall chimneys. Like other old homes along Orange Avenue, a portico was added to accommodate an automobile years later. J.T. Love was a prominent businessman in Floral City who owned grocery stores, meat markets, and a drugstore.

33

This impressive folk-Victorian house with an added tower was once a showpiece for the community. It was constructed in the 1880s west of the intersection of US 41 and Orange Avenue on Bedford Road. It was originally built for the superintendent of the Hines phosphate mine, part of the Mutual Mining Company. Later, it was bought by O.F. Roux, who brought his extended family to Floral City in 1907. Several generations of the Roux family lived here and became prominent in community life. Unfortunately, as the photograph below shows, this magnificent house was later abandoned, allowed to fall into disrepair, and eventually lost.

Built in 1908, this wood-frame house with battered columns is a variation of the Bungalow style, and typical of the period, it has no closets. It was built by Irwin and Billie Tooke, members of a prominent family of farmers and merchants who settled very early in the Floral City area. It was later owned by William Spivey and his wife, Estelle Spivey, who was John Paul Formy-Duval's great-granddaughter.

This beautiful two-story Classic Revival house was constructed in the early 1900s by local builder Mr. Dawsey. It is unlike all other remaining historic houses in Floral City and therefore makes an important contribution to the rural scenery. The house has passed through several ownerships over the years and has recently undergone a complete renovation.

These two photographs show the Classic Revival house of Joe Metz Sr. (above, left) and his wife, Ann (above, center). The other man is unidentified. It was probably constructed in the late 1800s because the detached kitchen building shown above is indicative of that early-style architecture. This farmhouse was located on their property adjacent to the northern shoreline of the Floral City Pool of Lake Tsala Apopka. They produced a large and successful citrus grove, which was eventually destroyed by successive hard freezes in the mid-1980s. The buildings and the grove are now gone, but the property is still owned by the Metz family.

The Jones House, another folk-Victorian structure, was located on the southwest corner of Magnolia Avenue and Great Oaks Drive. It was built before 1892 by C.G. Watson, Floral City's marshal at one time, and was well maintained by succeeding generations of the family, including the Joneses, until it burned in the late 1980s.

This attractive, Bungalow-style house was built by M.M. Smoak in 1924. It is one of the most visible historic homes in Floral City because of its central location on Route 41. Smoak owned a blacksmith shop next door at the northwest corner of the intersection of Route 41 and Orange Avenue.

This unique Victorian-style residence, known as the Jont Knight house, is composed of three structures interconnected by breezeways. The original structure was built in the 1880s. Knight bought the property in 1905 and added two more structures that he moved here from Brooksville, placing them on either side of the preexisting house. It now houses the Florida Artists Gallery, located just west of the main intersection. At one time, a phosphate mine railroad spur passed very close by the house.

This wood-frame, rectangular house was built in 1911 for Frank and Cora Morris. It has very high ceilings and a Corbel chimney. Morris was a crane operator at a local phosphate mine until it went out of business and held numerous other jobs, including Citrus County sheriff from 1948 to 1952. The house was restored by its new owners to its original state in the early 2000s.

Built around 1900 by a Mr. Durant, this charming rectangular wood-frame house was next to the railroad and used as a boardinghouse for phosphate workers. It was later owned by the Roux and Reid families. It sat abandoned for several years but recently was saved from destruction and completely restored in 2010.

While nearly all the other historic homes in Floral City were constructed with wood, this house is a masonry structure reminiscent of the architectural style made popular during the Florida realty boom of the 1920s. It was built in 1925 for real estate developer B.T. Keating, and its Spanish Colonial style, complete with terra-cotta roof tiles, makes it unique within the historic district.

Solomon D. Moon, one of the first people to settle in Floral City, was a farmer, civic leader, state representative, and real estate developer. He built this imposing two-story American foursquare house for his growing family in 1893, the same year the railroad came through town. It has been restored in keeping with the shingles and paint color of the original house.

This unique board-and-batten house, with its large, flat roof and sectional open porches, was built around 1900 and still stands at the southeast corner of Great Oaks Drive and Magnolia Avenue. Originally known as the Giddens House, for its first owner, it is reminiscent of the pioneer era. The house has changed hands several times and is now unfortunately empty and in a state of disrepair.

James A. Hampton arrived in Floral City before the Civil War. He married John Paul Formy-Duval's daughter Mary Jane and procured much of the land around Lake Hampton, where he established an orange grove. His grove was destroyed by the big freeze of 1894–1895, but unlike many other growers, he quickly replanted and started anew. Their beautiful folk-Victorian house, built in the 1880s, survived nearly a century but is now gone.

Highway U.S. 41 looking south at Floral City, Fla.

Whitacre's Grill, made up of two attached structures, was built in the early 1920s on the northeast corner of the main intersection. This 1940s photograph faces south on US 41. It was originally a combination gas station and restaurant, but the building complex has changed hands and uses several times since then. Even so, it is still called the Whitacre Building by locals.

This building at the northwest corner of the main intersection was built during the phosphate boom. It originally housed Smoak's Blacksmith shop and became this Texaco garage and bus station in the 1920s. It held the town's first public restroom. In recent years, it was called the Trading Post, but it has been closed since 1980.

These two views of the northeast corner of the main intersection show how things changed from the early 1940s to the early 1980s. Whitacre's Grill and Service Station became Holland's Feed Store, and the gas pumps were taken out. Note how the windows and doorways were altered. In recent years, it has housed a feed store, glass and mirror shop, used furniture store, pawn shop, carpet store, ice cream and sandwich shop, and a motorcycle shop. The old brick building is unchanged apart from the addition of an awning. Likewise, it has undergone numerous changes in occupancy over the years. The pharmacy had a wooden parapet wall added to it but otherwise is unchanged. The large, dark, wooden building above, which became Snyder's One Stop, burned down in 1949.

Unfortunately, about a dozen of the live oak trees on the north side of Orange Avenue at the eastern entrance to Floral City were cut down many years ago by a property owner when he planted an orange grove next to the road (above). The trees created too much shade for his small grove. Many of the lost live oak trees were later replaced by the townspeople after the grove was destroyed by a hard freeze. Floral City residents have fought hard to protect their live oak trees ever since. The gateway sign was erected in 2003 at the eastern end of Orange Avenue to welcome people to Floral City.

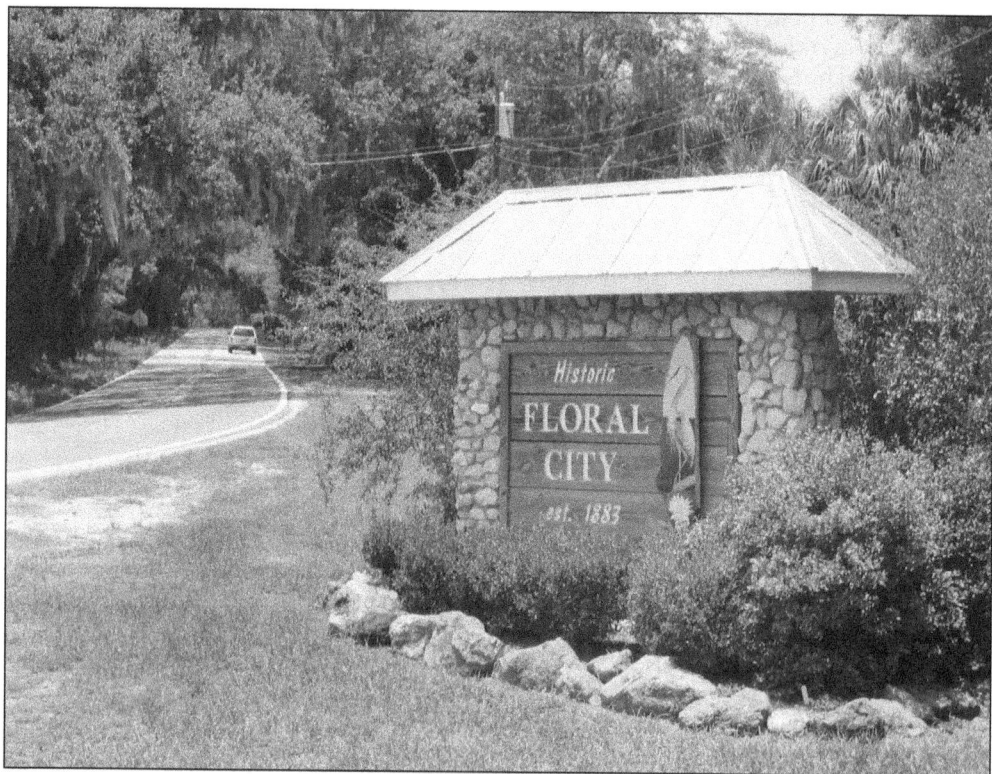

Three

MAKING A LIVING

A few bottles are all that remain of the Floral City Big Four Soda Works factory. The building was located on the south side of East Orange Avenue, just west of present-day US 41, and was in operation during Floral City's phosphate boom. These three bottles date from the turn of the 20th century and were hand-blown in molds.

Cattle were always a commodity in the state, especially during the Civil War, when Florida provided most of the beef for the Confederate war effort. Many Confederate veterans worked in the annual cattle drives, such as this modern one south of Floral City, which moved the cattle from central and north Florida down to the ship-loading pens at Punta Rassa, near Fort Myers. An anti-fence-cutting law was passed in 1868, but cattle were still allowed to graze on unfenced land, including roadways, which increasingly caused deadly accidents. A fencing law went into effect in 1950 that decreed cattle could no longer roam freely along state roads or within incorporated communities. One can still find the hoof impressions of meandering cattle on some of the very old sections of concrete sidewalk along Orange Avenue.

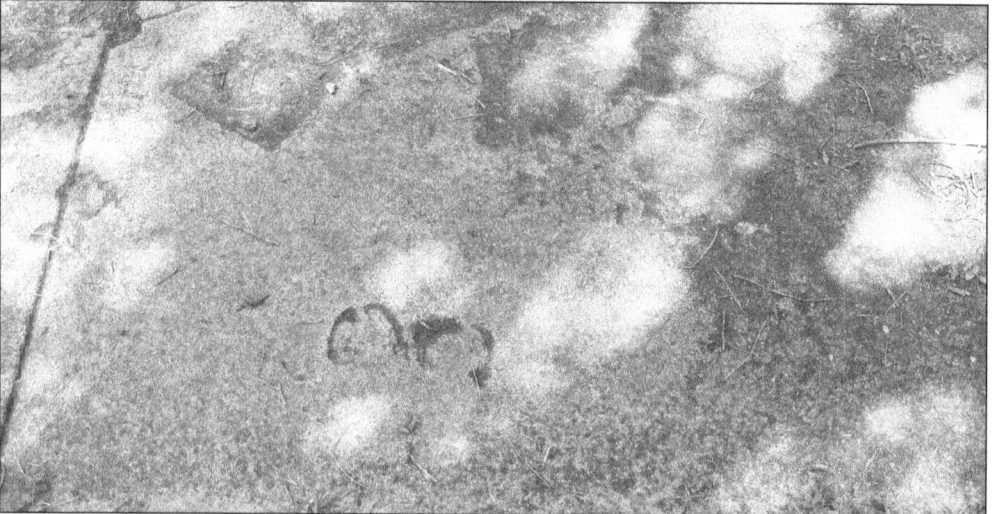

The Pyles brothers, Sam and James, operated a citrus plantation at Cove Bend on the Withlacoochee River. They shipped their fruit and locally produced molasses directly from their own pier, rather than carrying it by wagon overland to Floral City for shipment. This warehouse, which included upstairs living quarters, sat right on the pier.

The first electric wires were strung in Citrus County in 1913. Electricity was supplied by the Camp Phosphate Company, who operated the Dunnellon Hydro Dam power plant on the Withlacoochee River near Inglis. This photograph shows the electrical substation near Floral City in 1914, which provided electricity to central Citrus County. Telephone poles and wires were also erected at this time, linking Floral City's eight subscribers with the East Florida Telephone Company.

Built in 1883, now at 8212 East Orange Avenue, this house was the first post office in Floral City. It originally stood at the intersection of Orange Avenue and Baker Street. Postmaster James Fleming operated from a back room until the official post office was moved to the nearby Bushnell Hotel. This building was relocated to its current site in the early 1900s and used as a boardinghouse.

W.A. Bushnell, the postmaster after the post office was relocated to the rear of the Bushnell Hotel, poses at his desk. The Bushnell Hotel was located behind the present-day convenience store on Route 41, between Orange Avenue and Magnolia Avenue.

Floral City's post office was housed in this former bank building when this photograph was taken in 1920. Postmaster Mattie D. Perry stands in the center with Mrs. W.R. Townsend (right), the assistant postmaster. The third person is unidentified. Miss Mattie, as she was called by everyone in Floral City, was town postmaster for nearly 40 years. She was often seen wheeling the day's mail into the post office for sorting. Local kids often helped her wheel the cart from the train station to the post office, where she would reward them with a piece of candy.

The Floral City Drug Store was located on the north side of Orange Avenue next door to the brick post office building, near the intersection of Orange Avenue and Route 41. Louie Huot Castel, the son of owner John W. Castel, stands to the right of two unidentified people in front of the store in 1928.

This concrete block building, with an old-fashioned parapet wall, dates to the early 1940s. It stands on the north side of Orange Avenue, next to the Withlacoochee State Trail. It was originally King's Groceries before becoming Fay's Market. Owner Fay Metz and her son Jim open up the store in this photograph. She moved her market across the street in 1967, and this was converted to a garden shop and later a motorcycle shop.

The above image, possibly from the 1920s, shows Love's Market, owned by J.T. Love, who sold groceries and gasoline for 47 years. The small building with the porch roof in the background was John Landrum's barbershop. The market was also the main butcher shop for the town, and here J.B. King (left) and J.T. Love (right) cut up an impressive side of beef. Notice the palm growing through the boards in the upper left. King bought the store many years later, and it became known as King's Groceries.

This small general and grocery store, built in the early 1900s, was owned by Flora and Marion Myers. The exterior photograph was taken sometime after 1962, when the white Masonic Lodge building on the left was constructed. Myers also had a hauling business, and his truck can be seen in the background. The interior view, from 1949, shows that its long, narrow, rectangular shape allowed for an impressive amount of goods to be offered. As customers shop, Flora and Marion stand on the right. The quaint little store with the false front was torn down in the mid-1960s and replaced by a much larger concrete block building, currently a hardware store.

Several major oil companies were represented in Floral City in the past. For many years, Clarence Peters owned this Pure Oil service station, shown here in the late 1960s or early 1970s, on the southeast corner of the main intersection. The fuel dispensary was removed in the 1970s, and the station became a tire shop. It is now once again a service station, but it does not sell gas.

Midge and Maurice Johnson built this combination grocery store, gas station, and restaurant south of the main intersection on Route 41 in 1950. Bill and Marty Daniels, shown here in the 1960s, converted it into Daniel's Bar. It also served as a Trailways bus depot, photography shop, and bait shop. In the 1970s, it became Miss Kitty's Bar and then Bart's Place. Since 1984, it has been an antiques and collectibles store.

John Paul Formy-Duval established one of the first citrus groves in the region on Duval Island. The above image, from C.B. Colby's 1884 photograph cards, shows Formy-Duval's citrus trees prospering, a decade before the big freeze of 1894–1895 destroyed them. He sold the agricultural land to D.A. Tooke, who struggled for years to reestablish the grove, eventually giving up and selling the island in 1925 to James Ferris, who, with his son L.G. "Doc" Ferris, wanted to develop an 18-hole golf course. Doc inherited the island two years later and decided to grow citrus instead. By the time his grove started thriving, the fruit picking was done primarily by migrant farm workers (below), who arrived at harvest time and lived temporarily in barracks on his property. Note the oil heaters used to help protect the trees and fruit during freezes.

PICKING ORANGES   FERRIS GROVE FLORAL CITY FLA.

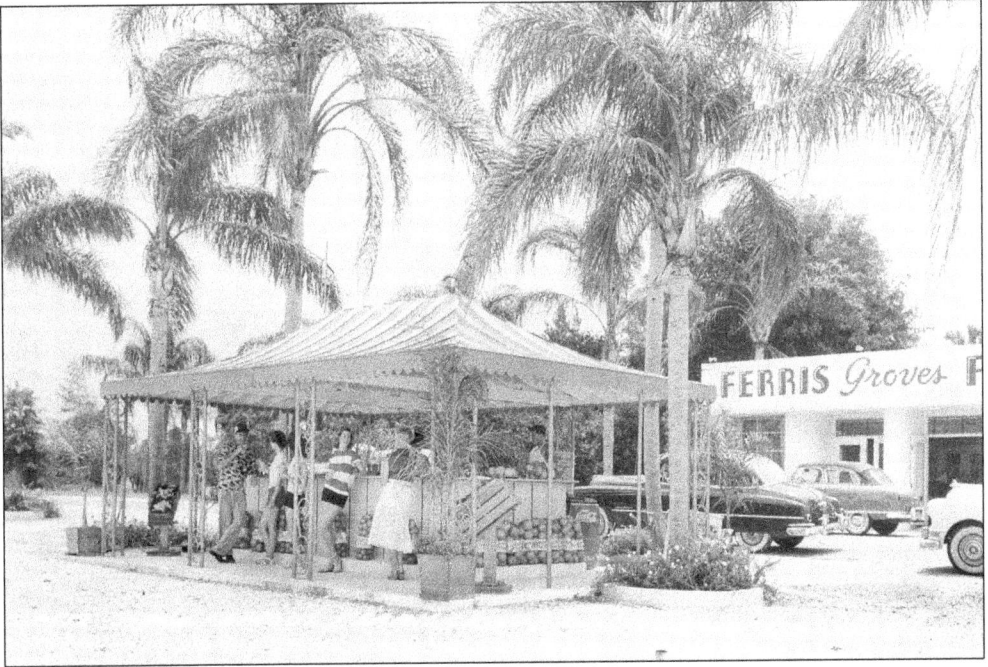

The Ferris fruit stand is perhaps the most recognizable structure in Floral City. Standing right alongside Route 41, its orange-and-white-striped roof is impossible to miss as people drive through town. The original fruit stand was a simple, open-sided, canvas-covered structure built in 1952. Years later, Doc Ferris replaced it with the larger brick and glass enclosure that still stands today. Doc's fruit won many awards for its high quality, and he was quick to take advantage of this in his promotions. Early on, he coined the slogan "Finer Fruit" for his citrus. After continuing to win awards, he changed the slogan to "Finest Fruit in Florida" and finally to "The Finest Name in Citrus."

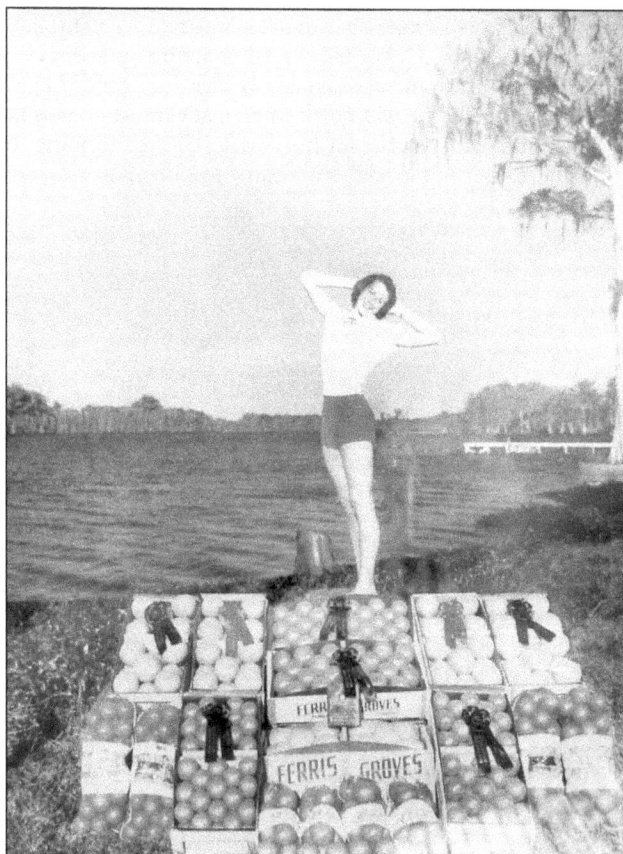

Doc Ferris was notorious for employing attractive young women to promote his fruit. Knowing this would be a good way to get attention for his product, he erected several roadside billboards and printed advertisements with bathing suit–clad beauties holding and admiring Ferris citrus fruit. This large outdoor advertisement was actually a three-dimensional covered stage with plywood figures. It was located across the road from the Ferris packinghouse. The unidentified young woman with the citrus fruit and numerous award ribbons is standing near the shore of Lake Tsala Apopka on the Ferris property with the Ferris pier in the background.

The Ferris groves were planted according to the lay of the land, so there were no long rows of trees but instead many different sections, with trees aligned in various compass directions. Of the approximately 500 acres that form Duval Island, Ferris eventually planted 350 acres in citrus trees. The soil of Duval Island was formed over thousands of years from the decayed vegetation of primeval forests, which made it a superior substrate for growing citrus trees. Only about 15 percent of Florida's citrus groves are located on similar "hammock land." In the 1950s, Doc had a canal dredged along the east side of the island and the excavated muck was spread around the groves, enriching the soil even more.

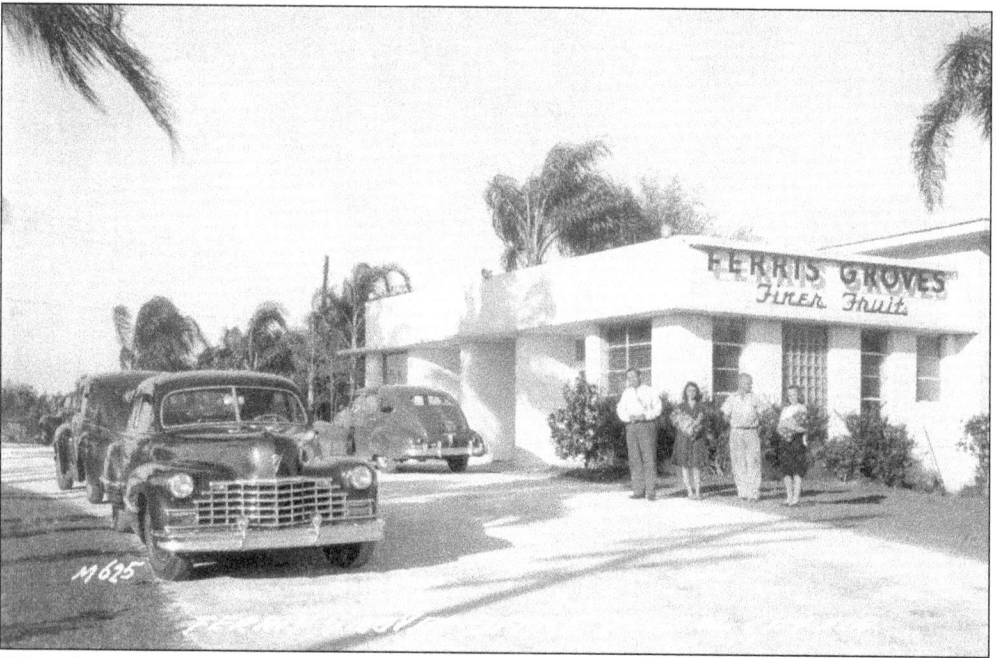

When his citrus trees began producing marketable fruit, Doc Ferris realized he needed a special building to accommodate shipping the products. In 1941, he built a large packinghouse on property he owned along Route 41, just north of the main intersection of Floral City. Ferris Groves became the major employer in Floral City, with a half-dozen full-time workers who trimmed, fertilized, and watered. During the harvest season, 15 to 20 pickers were hired, and another 35 to 40 people worked in the packinghouse. By 1960, Ferris had an annual payroll of about $75,000. Below, Ferris holds a huge fake orange at right in front of this billboard, directly below the company logo, the Ferris wheel, which was invented by his great-uncle George Washington Gales Ferris.

Doc Ferris (right) and an unidentified young helper plant a grafted sapling in the grove in the 1950s. While the company was established in the 1930s, much of the land had to be cleared of its dense undergrowth and old trees before citrus trees could be planted. It took 25 years to remove the huge, ancient trees located in the zones Ferris wanted for his citrus.

Like many citrus growers, E.A. Zellner planted rows of sugar cane between his young trees, which provided extra income during fall season. This 1906 photograph shows a gathering of Zellner family members and friends squeezing sugar cane in a mule-driven Chattanooga mill. The cane juice was then boiled down to produce cane syrup. Only Eva May Baker, on the left, and Broadus Zellner, standing in the center, are identified.

A wind machine was erected by crane on the Metz citrus grove, near the north shore of the Floral City Pool of Lake Tsala Apopka, in the early 1960s. This was fairly new technology at the time but had already proven effective in giving extra protection to trees during extended hard freezes. The massive spinning propeller moved the surrounding air enough to counteract the typically still cold air that was more likely to freeze fruit solid and ruin it. But occasionally a freeze is so severe, the wind machines are insufficient to protect the fruit, and that was the case at the Metz grove. Note that the orange trees are long gone and the surrounding area has grown up in laurel oaks (below). The machine still stands, but now it is just an interesting relic.

The Floral City region's sandy, humic-rich, well-drained soil is ideal for citrus trees. Being north of the frost line insures that the fruit will experience occasional light frosts, which can increase the sugar content and sweetness of the fruit. However, hard freezes are dangerous because they can ruin the fruit and kill the trees, which happened here at the Ferris grove in the 1950s.

Commercial orange trees usually consist of sour orange rootstocks, with desired fruit-producing growth grafted onto the main stem just above the ground. The rootstocks can be grown from seeds, but the valuable fruit-producing plant parts must be taken from existing trees. Unfortunately, if a tree is destroyed by a freeze, the roots often resprout and produce multi-trunk trees with worthless sour fruit, like this one.

During the late 1800s and early 1900s, forestry was a big industry around Floral City. The most desired lumber came from ancient, giant bald cypress trees, once in abundance in the lake and riverine habitats. This giant somehow escaped the axes and still survives at Trails End. It is the sixth largest known specimen in Florida at about 90 feet tall and 27 feet in circumference.

Bald cypress wood is known as a superior, weather-resistant product that was traditionally used to make bent wood furniture. The Wilson family operated a bent wood furniture workshop in the c. 1895 Edwards-Puckett House, at the northwest end of Levy Lane, for many years. Their furniture was in high demand and was shipped all over the country. This cottage industry ended when the old house was demolished in 2009.

People collect Spanish moss, commonly used as stuffing for mattresses, throw pillows, and chair cushions, in the 1930s. The moss was put in huge piles and kept wet until the plant's outer sheath rotted off. This left behind a strong fiber that was used as a substitute for horsehair, cotton, and wool. In the mid-1930s, fiber sold for $1.50 to $2 per 100 pounds.

In the 1800s, Spanish moss was used as a substitute for wool. It was soaked to render the processed fibers into a flexible and soft material that could be woven into woolen-like blankets. The technique continued to be used on a small scale by backwoods people well into the 20th century. Dawn Klug, who lives near Floral City, is one of the few weavers still creating traditional moss blankets. (Courtesy of Dawn Klug.)

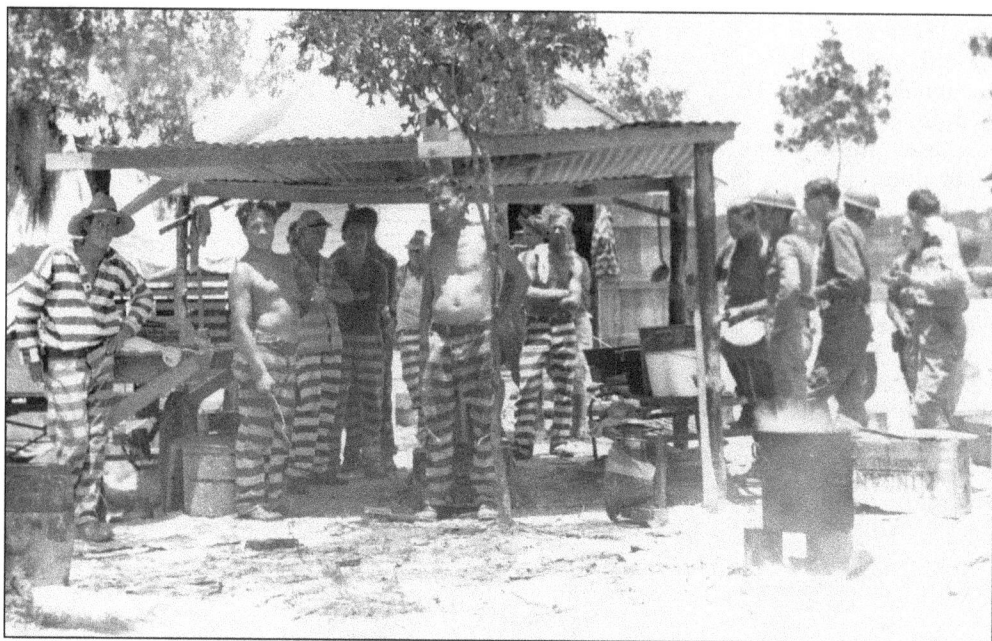

In 1919, the Florida road prison system was established and convicts were put to work cleaning and clearing roadways. Here, convicts work at a prison labor camp south of Floral City, perhaps near Brooksville. The Floral City road prison was located just east of town at the intersection of County Road 48 and County Road 39 (Istachatta Road). Initially, the convicts wore horizontal striped suits, but they were discontinued in 1937. The use of leg irons was eliminated in the mid-1940s, sweatboxes were terminated in 1958, and convict labor for roadwork was abolished in the 1960s. The Floral City road prison was turned over to the Florida Department of Transportation in the 1960s, which used it as a regional office and for equipment storage place until the 1990s. The old prison manager's residence (below) is the only remaining building. (Above, courtesy of Florida Archives.)

A valuable phosphate deposit was found near Floral City a few years before the big freeze of 1894–1895 devastated the citrus-dependent economy. It did not take long for the local economy to shift from citrus to the mining and export of phosphate, which is used in the production of synthetic fertilizer. The Cove Bend phosphate mine (above) was located just outside Floral City but had its company office in Inverness. One of the special tools of the phosphate industry was a unique style of wheelbarrow known as the "Georgia buggy," several of which are visible in these photographs. It was designed to dump its load off to the side rather than from the front, making it much easier to handle the rocks and small boulders.

Soon after hard rock phosphate was discovered in northern Florida, people flocked to the area hoping to make their fortunes. Within a very short period of time, geologists and prospectors swarmed the woods, making test drills and pits in search of valuable deposits. Mobile prospecting and drilling equipment were easily moved about, as this photograph from the early 1900s demonstrates. (Courtesy of US Geological Survey.)

Initially, hard rock phosphate mining was done by hand with picks and shovels under slave-like working conditions by poorly paid laborers. But by the early 1900s, most excavations were done by huge steam-powered shovels, such as this one working a phosphate deposit in 1907. This technology greatly improved efficiency and working conditions and reduced the need for unskilled labor. (Courtesy of US Geological Survey.)

The Bradley brothers, Peter and Robert, owned the Bradley Phosphate Mining Company and operated several mines, two of which are shown here, within a few miles south and west of Floral City. The company headquarters was in Floral City, and their family name is still very prominent in the area. There was once a small mining town called Bradleys, complete with a post office, located near the southern shore of Lake Bradley along Floral Park Road, just south of Floral City. The town of Bradleys no longer exists, but there is a tiny hamlet at the site along the aptly named Bradley Street.

The phosphate deposits were associated with limestone and covered with overburden that had to be removed to give access to the valuable rock, which created problems. Excavation pits often cut into the aquifer, which resulted in flooding, and barge-mounted dredges were necessary to scoop out the underwater phosphate deposits. Here, a mine dredge operates in a pit north of Floral City in 1919. Note the raised track used to move carts to and from the dredge. Below is a modern view of the rotting pilings in an abandoned flooded pit, now part of the Mutual Mine recreation area in the Withlacoochee State Forest. (Above, courtesy of US Geological Survey.)

Four

TOWN LIFE

The New Hope United Methodist Church was established in 1831, just 10 years after Florida became a US territory, making it one of the oldest continually operating Protestant congregations in Florida. The existing church, shown here, is the third structure used near this site as the congregation's house of worship.

The first New Hope United Methodist Church was a log building that was also used as a schoolhouse, a town hall, and a fortification against Indians. It burned down after 50 years, and this simple, rectangular wood-frame structure was built in 1886. The cemetery on the church grounds—barely visible to the left of the building—contains some of the earliest burials in Citrus County, dating to the mid-1800s. The interior of the church is seen here in the early 1900s. Although it was remodeled in 1940, the piano, much of the lumber, many of the pews, and the magnificent cast-iron heater stove were saved and incorporated into the present-day building.

In the early years, there was much undeveloped land in Floral City, and numerous parklike, oak-shaded open areas provided perfect picnic sites. This beautiful setting is near Lake Consuela, where the Baptist congregation often held services under the shade of live oaks. Note that all are dressed in their Sunday best and the ladies and children are seated on a church pew. The Floral City Baptist Church was later built on this spot in 1899. It is also the site of the Seminole village of Cho-illy-hadjo that existed when Spanish conquistadors first arrived in the region in the early 1500s. Local tradition holds that Lake Consuela was named by a Spanish conquistador pining for the love of a beautiful señorita back in Spain. But it was actually named by an early pioneer in the mid-1800s in honor of his daughter, who was known for her beauty.

The United Methodist Church of Floral City, on Marvin Avenue between Old Floral City Road and Church Street, was originally the Floral City Mission Church. It was built in 1884 by George Higgins and was part of a circuit system ministered by traveling pastors. Although a larger church was built next door in 1983, the original church is still in use and is a focal point of the historic neighborhood.

The Pleasant Hill Baptist Church at the intersection of Magnolia Avenue and Bedford Road, just off Route 41, was built around 1895. It is the oldest existing black congregation in Floral City and one of the two sites in Floral City designated as part of the Florida Black History Trail.

Four families got together in 1888 and built the Cove Bend Baptist Church of Jesus Christ. Services were only held every first Sunday of each month, and the pastor was paid $15 per month. The membership grew rapidly, and a decade later, a larger church was built in Floral City. Here, siblings Maurice Jr. and Carolyn Johnson pose in front of the old Cove Bend church.

Initially, the Floral City Baptist congregation met under the live oak trees near Lake Consuela, but in 1899, they hired George Higgins to build this wood-frame church on Magnolia Avenue and changed the name to First Baptist. This building was replaced in 1964 by the existing brick and masonry structure next to the original site, which was torn down in 1973.

The Mount Carmel Methodist congregation originated as an African Methodist Episcopal congregation in 1903. The early church had a large membership during the phosphate boom, but it dwindled to just a handful of members after the industry's collapse. This is perhaps the only surviving image of the magnificent original church, looking north along Route 41. Beyond the church structure, only partly visible on the left, are a couple of Cracker-style houses and a Ferris fruit sign, with Floral City in the distance. The building unfortunately deteriorated and was replaced with a much smaller church in 1967 (below), at which time the congregation became independent.

The Grace Temple Church of the Living God on Old Floral City Road originated as the St. Luke Baptist Church in 1904 but changed to its present affiliation in 1958. The original building was torn down in the 1960s, and a masonry and brick church was constructed. In 2001, this new matching church building was added to the complex. The previous church building is now a meeting hall.

The Church of Christ of Floral City was organized in 1910, but initially the members used the old school building to hold their services. Many years later, they switched to the Community House as a place to hold their services. In 1945, they built their first church, the existing concrete block structure on the corner of Marvin Avenue and Church Street.

Floral City children have had access to schooling since the town's inception, but the first few decades saw many changes in the school system. The first Floral City School was a shingle-covered, one-room structure at the intersection of Baker Street and Orange Avenue. It was replaced in 1884 with a two-room structure a few blocks closer to the steamboat dock at the corner of Jefferson and Duval Streets. That one was replaced with a third two-story school in 1897, on the north side of Marvin Avenue between Church and College Streets. These photographs show the fourth school, built in 1906. It was a large two-story building, one block farther west on Marvin Avenue. Initially, it had a bell tower, which was removed several years later after it was struck by lightning, and a portico was added.

First and second graders pose in front of the Floral City School in 1921. All of the children are well dressed for their official school portrait, but, with the exception of the boy sitting on the far left, they are all barefoot.

The fourth Floral City School, built by the Works Progress Administration (WPA), was condemned in the late 1930s, and classes were held in the Masonic Lodge building while a new school was constructed. Here, Rachel Roux and her elementary students pose in front of the Community House in the 1940–1941 school year. The new school was completed and ready for students when school began the next year.

The present-day school was opened in 1941, holding elementary and junior high classes. All high school classes had already been moved to Inverness. Local black children were bused to Inverness schools because of segregation laws. In 1970, the junior high classes were also moved to Inverness and integration became law. The school is located at the intersection of Old Floral City Road and Marvin Avenue, but it extends the entire width of the block all the way to Jefferson Avenue. Since 1970, this has been the only public elementary school in the southeastern quadrant of the county, and numerous school buses have long been necessary to get all the area's kids to and from classes, as one can infer from this 1970s photograph of Floral City school bus drivers.

Five

GETTING AROUND

In the late 1920s or early 1930s, a speeding steam locomotive heading southward to Lakeland derailed a short distance south of Floral City and plowed into the embankment after traveling more than 200 feet off the track. It was a dramatic event, but there were no fatalities and little damage was sustained.

The *Reindeer* operated on the Withlacoochee River between Lake Panasoffkee and Pemberton's Ferry (now Croom) in the late 1800s. She also made side trips via the Orange State Canal to the boat pier at Floral City. At 10 feet wide and 60 feet long, she was very maneuverable, with a flat bottom for shallow draft, and was powered by a single steam-driven stern paddle wheel.

Pictured in the 1890s, the steamboat *John L. Inglis* enters the Orange State Canal at the present-day location of the bridge to Duval Island. The loading pier was a short distance away at the end of Aroostook Way, which was once the main avenue of commerce for the town. Steamboats and paddle wheels were used to haul citrus fruit, lumber, turpentine, produce, and passengers.

The local citrus industry received a tremendous boost when the South Florida Railroad, part of the Henry B. Plant System, was extended through Floral City in 1893. A portion of the train depot, built a few years later, is on the right in this photograph, next to the Model T. The railway soon became the fastest and most efficient mode of transport for mail, lumber, phosphate, dry goods, perishable goods, and of course, people. In spite of its meager beginnings, the railroad helped Floral City grow to be the largest town in Citrus County before the end of the 19th century. However, the citrus boom came to an abrupt end two years later when the big freeze of 1894–1895 wiped out nearly all the local groves, and the phosphate industry quickly took its place in the local economy. The coming of the railroad, combined with the disastrous freeze and the resulting collapse of the citrus industry, brought about an end to the steamboat era in Floral City.

The Floral City depot, with its unique gable decoration, was constructed in the mid-1890s, shortly after the rails were laid down in eastern Citrus County. It was important for both the citrus-based economy and during the phosphate boom but lost its usefulness as the population dwindled and trains no longer stopped in Floral City. It was demolished in the early 1950s.

I. Snyder, a well-known muralist who created many local works, painted this dynamic mural on a historic 1940s building that has housed a grocery store, a repair shop, and the present motorcycle shop. The mural is just a few yards from where the Floral City Depot stood for more than a half-century.

The railroad that passed through Floral City was within the Ocala district of the Atlantic Coast Line system. This track line extended nearly 140 miles, from Lakeland to High Springs, but was peculiar in that it consisted of a single track for 19 miles from Lakeland to Vitus, a double track for 60 miles from Vitus passing through Floral City to Dunnellon, and a single track for 59 miles from Dunnellon to High Springs. Floral City section foreman W.G. Puckett (below, left) inspected the double tracks just north of town in the early 1950s. After a train wreck near Floral City in 1956, one of the tracks was removed so that the entire length from Lakeland to Dunnellon was a single track.

Floral City was the site of one of the worst train disasters in the history of Florida. Early in the morning on October 18, 1956, two fully laden diesel-powered trains traveling at maximum allowable speed collided head-on just south of Floral City. A northbound train from Lakeland had been switched over to the southbound track at Croom in order to bypass a stalled train and run "against the current" as far as Dunnellon. It was discovered later that a southbound train had already passed Dunnellon but had not yet passed Croom, and last-minute efforts to stop the collision failed. The three crew members aboard the southbound train were all killed instantly, but two of the three crew members of the northbound train survived because they had a few seconds to react to the impending crash knowing they were going against traffic.

Nick Metz relaxes on the hood of his 1927 Ford Model T convertible. He was a flamboyant member of the Metz family of Floral City. Many years earlier, he had been an orange grower in Mexico but was run out of that country by Pancho Villa. Metz came to Floral City to be near his brother Joe, another citrus grower, and established an orange grove of his own near Moon Lake.

From left to right, Ed Hooker, Gene Consadine, Jim Metz, and an unidentified man nearly hidden from view set off for a hunting trip in the 1940s. Metz's converted flatbed Ford Model T made an ideal vehicle to transport all their hunting and camping equipment. Note the extended vertical exhaust pipe that allowed the vehicle to drive through deep water.

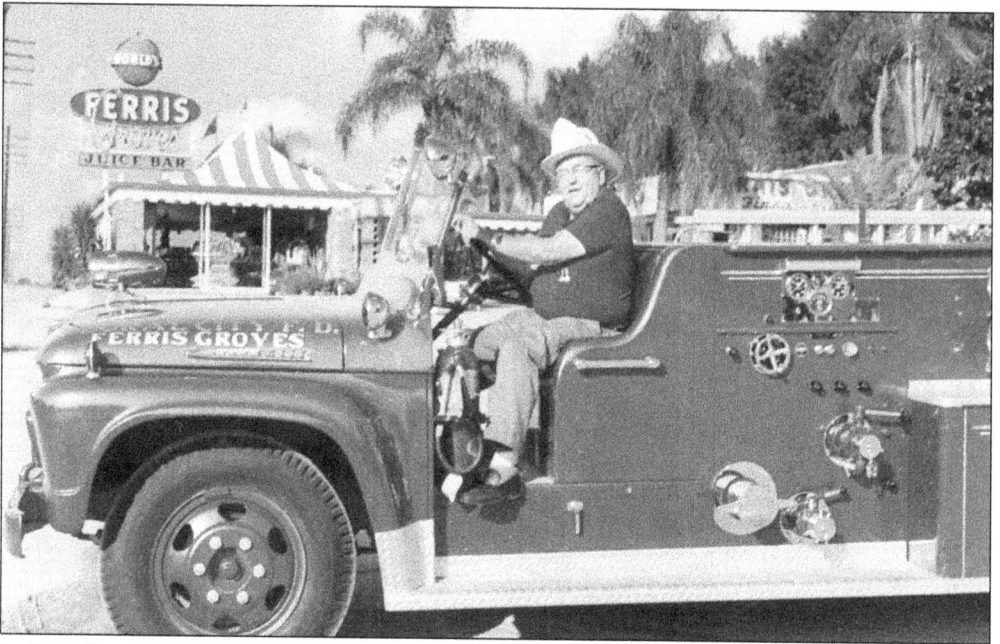

In 1961, Doc Ferris and Floral City fire chief Dave Anderson decided the town needed a fire truck and a fire station. Ferris purchased a fire truck in Kenosha, Wisconsin, and had a friend drive it to Florida. Ferris followed in his Cadillac convertible. When they reached Inverness, the Citrus High School Band welcomed them. The truck was escorted to Floral City by the Inverness fire truck and sheriff's cars.

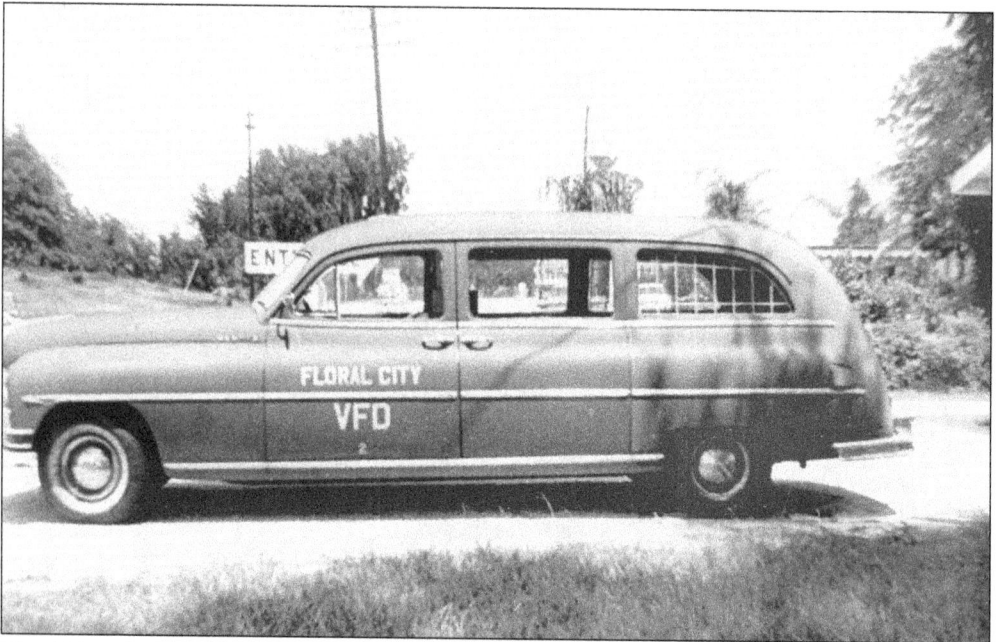

Floral City also got a full-time ambulance in 1961 in order to transfer people to the Citrus Memorial Hospital in Inverness, which opened in 1957. This was the first healthcare institution in Citrus County; it eliminated the need for residents to travel all the way to Tampa or Ocala for serious medical treatment. Note the Ferris fruit stand in the background.

Teenagers Bob Metz and Earl Zellner ride on a classic Allis-Chalmers tractor on the Joseph Metz citrus grove in the mid-1940s. Neither of them yet had a driver's license, but the younger Metz often drove the tractor, helping his grandfather among the orange trees.

An unidentified teenage bicyclist poses in the late 1920s on the Zellner property near Floral City. This type of bicycle, with pneumatic tires and a chain-driven rear wheel, was developed around 1900 and was superior to the earlier kind that had a huge front wheel driven by fixed pedals. Bicycles have long been popular in Floral City and are used extensively nowadays on the Withlacoochee State Trail, which passes through town.

The earliest bridges across the Withlacoochee River were wooden structures constructed by the US military, which were destroyed and rebuilt during the Second Seminole War. They were later replaced with stronger bridges like this iron and wood structure that once stood at Istachatta. Remnants of the bridge pilings can still be seen, but today the concrete spans of Routes 48 and 476 are the only local Withlacoochee River bridges.

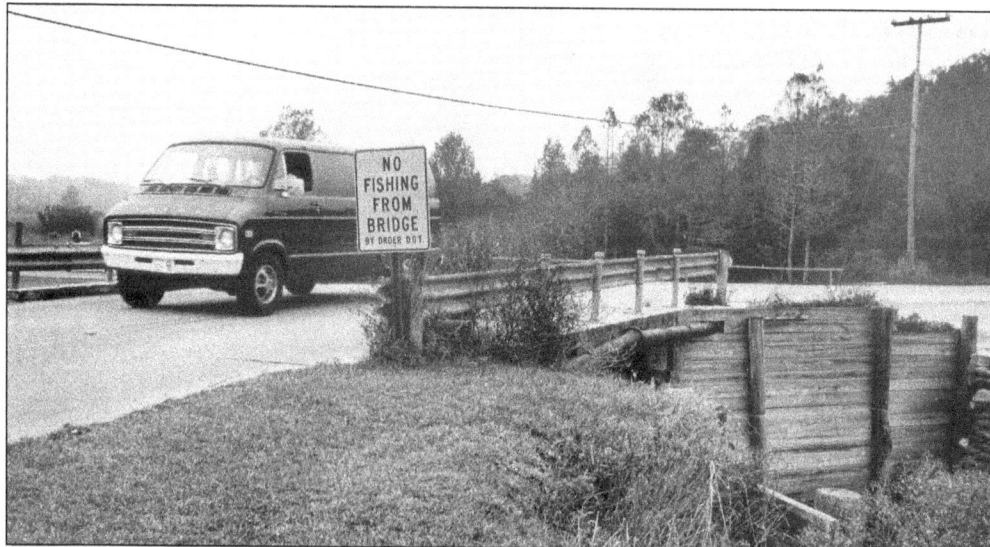

When this photograph of the old Duval Island Bridge was taken in 1979, some of the pilings had rotted out and sections of the wooden revetment wall were damaged. This deteriorated state allowed some of the packed earth to collapse into the Orange State Canal, and the resulting erosion is visible in the lower right. In 1981, the bridge was rebuilt and all the wood was replaced with poured concrete and limestone boulders.

Six

LEISURE TIME

The New England Hotel, constructed in 1884, was one of Floral City's first commercial buildings, part of the original town center near Tsala Apopka Lake. It was popular and successful when transportation was primarily by way of paddleboats and horse-drawn carriages. But when boat traffic was replaced by the railroads, the town center was moved closer to the railway line, and the hotel lost importance and eventually disappeared.

The Commercial Hotel on Orange Avenue was built in 1884. This beautiful folk-Victorian structure was the private residence of James and Celeste (Formy-Duval) Baker. It was regarded as the finest home in Floral City and was originally located at the corner of Orange Avenue and Church Street. After 1893, it was moved to its present location and converted into a hotel. It is now once again a private residence.

The Magnolia Hotel was located next to the Commercial Hotel on the north side of Orange Avenue. It was a popular hotel with businessmen associated with the phosphate industry, but it later became an annex to its next-door neighbor. Sadly, the hotel was torn down in the early 1970s, and the site is now occupied by a convenience store.

The Sunshine Lodge was established in the 1950s on the west shore of the Floral City Pool and is typical of the efficiency-type cottages that were once common throughout Florida, where people came to relax and escape the northern winter. It is still in operation and rents out several cottages.

The Moonrise Resort, located on Lake Tsala Apopka just north of Floral City, began operation in the early 1950s. The main clients are winter visitors from the north—affectionately referred to as "snowbirds" by the locals—who typically spend several weeks or even the entire winter here. Today, some people even live here as permanent renters. This postcard from the 1960s shows the resort from the lake.

COMMUNITY HOUSE- FLORAL CITY- FLA.
M1436

In 1929, land was given to the Floral City Woman's Club for its new meetinghouse. They deeded the property to Citrus County in 1938; this structure was built by the WPA. Named the Community House, it has been the main setting for local community events ever since. Native limestone from area mines was used in its construction. It is a well-built structure and little has changed in the 60 years between these two photographs. The only difference is that the drive-through portico in the 1950 photograph above is now an elevated porch. It is owned by the Citrus County government but for decades has been leased to the Lions Club, which offers it up for local events.

The Floral City Woman's Club took over the Lighthouse realty office at the southwest corner of the main intersection for its meetinghouse in the mid-1920s. The organization began as a Home Extension Club but became a Federated Woman's Club in 1924. In 1927, representatives from all the women's clubs in and around Citrus County posed for a picture at their regional meeting.

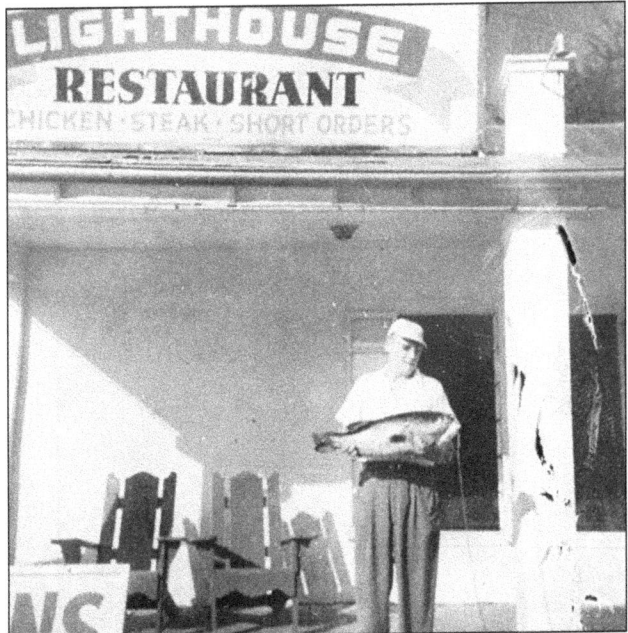

The Floral City Woman's Club was sold in the late 1930s and converted into the Lighthouse Restaurant. Here, the restaurant owner, a Mr. Patton, poses with an impressive largemouth bass caught in the nearby lake system. Many years later, the restaurant was changed into the Lighthouse Pub. The lighthouse structure was removed in the 1960s, and in 2006, the old building was so deteriorated it had to be razed.

WARNING

DEADLY POISON

Moonshine Liquor

Being Distributed Locally

DO NOT DRINK ANY Type of BOOTLEG LIQUOR regardless of source DEADLY POISONOUS Lead Salts are being found in WHITE LIQUOR. This poison can cause DEATH or serious illness as much as a year after drinking.

The next SMALL DRINK May Bring the amount of Lead Salts in the Body to the concentration point necessary to cause DEATH!

Dr. J. W. R. NORTON
State Health Director

Floral City had a serious liquor problem in the early 1900s, aggravated by the large population of unskilled and uneducated workers in town. There was considerable tension within the community over the enforcement of liquor laws, but illegal moonshine stills and rum-running endured virtually unabated. This small still from the 1920s was used during Prohibition and afterwards as well. Poorly monitored production could result in dangerous wood alcohol, which could lead to blindness and death. The lead solder used to make this still also produced poisonous alcohol, as this 1920s poster warns.

The Wishing Stone Tavern, a few miles north of town on Route 41, was established in the early 1930s by the Smoak family. It has changed very little in the ensuing decades, except for a new roof, a couple more stars in the flag, and the satellite dish in this modern photograph. The name came from a limestone boulder just outside the tavern. Legend says that if one rubs the smooth, rounded boulder while making a wish, it will come true. The remnants of the historic Wishing Stone Cottages are directly across the highway.

Several small cottages were built here along what is now Route 41 in the mid-1920s, on what was a fish camp for Lake Magnolia. In the 1930s, several small houses from nearby Floral City were added to the complex. This was one of the first motels for the burgeoning auto-oriented Florida tourist trade and included a communal bathhouse and a restaurant. Six of the historic cottages still exist.

From left to right, John Ogden, holding a small .22-caliber rifle; his mother, Kate Fellows Ogden; Vera Ogden Rawls; and Hazel Ogden Bell pose while on a shopping trip in downtown Floral City around 1900. A part of the early business district is visible, before much of it was destroyed by the great fire of 1920.

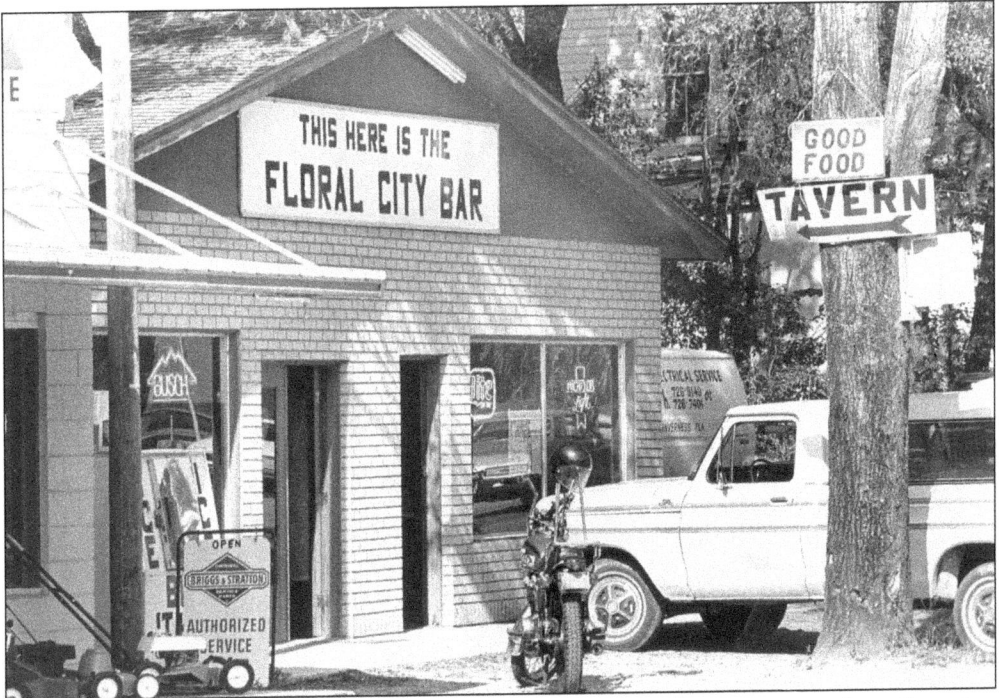

In 1971, this brick addition was added to R and L Repair, a lawn mower and small-engine repair shop, in order to establish a new lawn and garden center. However, the new business was unsuccessful, and the addition was soon sold off and converted to a popular tavern called This Here is the Floral City Bar. The tavern quickly became famous for its long curving bar and excellent hamburgers. In the above photograph, one can see the corner of R and L Repair on the left and the old Commercial Hotel building, now a private residence, behind the trees on the right. About 10 years later, the bar's name was changed to the Shamrock Inn, which it is still called today.

Floral City is nearly surrounded by fresh water, including the Floral City Pool of the Tsala Apopka lake system, Lakes Bradley and Consuela, several other smaller ponds, lakes, marshes, swamps, and flooded abandoned phosphate pits. All this water as well as the Withlacoochee River three miles east of town has provided an ideal situation for human habitation and recreation. The subjects in this photograph card from C.B. Colby's 1884 set carefully posed for the long-exposure style of box camera used in the day. There are no ripples on the surface or any other significant movement, which would have made the photograph even blurrier than it is.

This 1920s photograph of Charlie and Maggie Marsh shows that even in those early days, there were already thick growths of introduced water hyacinths in the Tsala Apopka lake system. It is believed this attractive, but a nuisance, floating water plant from tropical South America was first introduced into the United States in 1884 at an exposition in New Orleans. It soon made its way into the northern Florida waterways from private ponds and began covering and jamming lakes and rivers all over the Southeast. The Ferris Canal (right) on the east side of Duval Island was almost completely choked in the 1970s. For more than a century, various government agencies have been engaged in a never-ending battle against this formidable green adversary.

Three rental boats are tied up at the Trails End fishing camp in the 1950s. The camp, which rents cottages, is at the end of East Trails End Road, a few miles east of Floral City. These boats are good examples of the flat-bottomed, square-sterned rowboats popular in west central Florida throughout the late 19th and early 20th centuries. Very few of these early boats still survive, but low water levels in the early 2000s exposed three rowboats buried for decades in the shoreside river mud near Trails End camp. The mud had both hidden and preserved the boats, and the one seen below was donated to the Floral City Heritage Council.

Boswell's Island - LAKE TSALA APOPKA FLORAL City

This 1884 C.B. Colby photograph shows that small boats were a means of transportation in the early, water-oriented world of Floral City. This man, perhaps one of the Boswell brothers, is carrying cargo and holding a paddle in a canoe-like wooden boat. Boswells Island, now known as Johnson Island, is visible in the background. A very early citrus grove is on the island amongst the large trees.

Another 1884 C.B. Colby promotional photograph shows two well-dressed but unidentified gentlemen joking around in a rowboat surrounded by water lilies, with Willow Island in the background.

Alligators were an important game animal in days past, as they provided valuable skins and meat. Unfortunately, hunting pressure nearly eliminated them from local waters until they were given federal protection in 1962. Today, they are again common within Floral City's lakes, ponds, canals, swamps, and marshes and throughout the Withlacoochee River system. They are an integral part of the local environment, and most residents enjoy their presence.

Ebert Castel (aiming the rifle) and his father, Louie Huot Castel, hunt alligators in Lake Tsala Apopka. The photograph was set up with a dead alligator because no live, wild alligator would let them get this close without bolting for deeper water. This late-1920s image shows the steamboat pier that extended into the lake from the end of Aroostook Way.

An unidentified toddler sits in a rowboat pulled ashore in the rushes along the lake about 1890. The child's parents had probably been out collecting water lilies, a popular activity at the time. People would place water lily blossoms in bowls of water and spread them around the house to spruce things up.

Joseph Metz Jr. shows off the day's catch of about 10 largemouth bass and one chain pickerel, caught in the Floral City Pool of Lake Tsala Apopka in the 1930s. It would have been easy to catch that many in a day because the water was clear, the bottom was sandy, and there were few nonnative noxious waterweeds.

Hunting and fishing have always been popular in Floral City. The above image, from the early 1900s, shows brothers Joseph and Nick Metz home from a wild turkey hunt (Joseph and his wife, Anne, are on the left and Nick and daughter Kate are on the right). They are posing in front of Joseph and Anne's home. In the image at left, from the 1940s, Fred Wiggens (left) and Joseph Metz's son Jim pose in front of the historic Duval House—then owned by the Metzes—after another successful wild turkey hunt. Part of the front porch is on the left and a portion of the large, cement-covered brick cistern is on the right. Wild turkeys are still fairly common around Floral City.

Siblings Lillian, Pamela, Faye, and Joe Ann Black play on the bank of Lake Tsala Apopka with a patient pony in the 1950s. The water level was extraordinarily low at this time, producing extensive beaches that were popular with the locals. A few relic pilings from the old steamboat pier at the end of Aroostook Way can be seen in the background. Nothing remains of the pier today.

Brothers Phil and John Zellner, Lucille Carroll, and jockey Leroy (surname unknown) pose in the winner's circle with a first place trophy after winning a horse race in Ocala about 1970. The beautiful quarter horse's name was Joe Love II, and he raced all over the state, winning several races. John Zellner claimed that it got to the point where other owners would not race their horses against him.

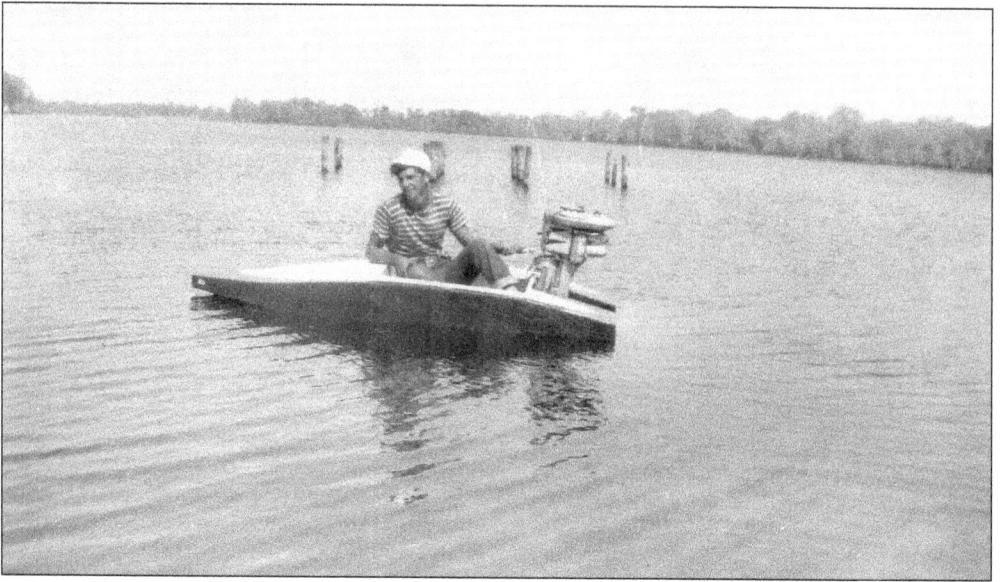

Bob Metz built this small speedboat out of wooden frame boards and plywood in the 1940s. It only held one person but was fast enough to pull a water-skier. Some rotten pilings from the old steamboat pier poke out of the water in the background. Below, Bob Metz (far left), his future wife, Betty Rawls, and several friends pose at a popular gathering spot on the shore of Lake Tsala Apopka, with Duval Island in the background. Behind them is the same little boat with a different engine. Metz was given this jalopy-like truck, a converted 1927 Ford Model A automobile, as payment for work he did on a house along Orange Avenue. Surprisingly, he kept it running for several more years.

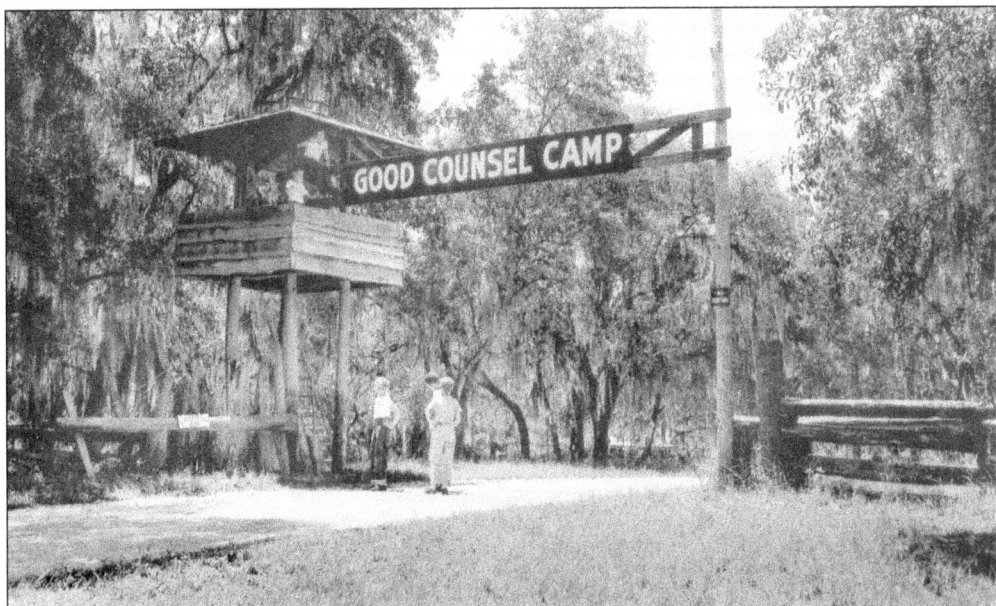

The Good Counsel Camp is a popular summer camp for boys and girls from ages seven to 15. Started by Msgr. George W. Cummings, it has been operated by the Catholic Diocese of St. Petersburg since 1948. The camp sits in a large, wooded area adjacent to Lake Tsala Apopka, a few miles north of Floral City, and is part of the Catholic Church's youth ministry program.

Three young boys spend an afternoon fishing with cane poles from a rowboat in the Withlacoochee River. This idyllic, undated photograph may have been taken near the Trails End fishing camp, just downstream from the bridge on Route 48.

LAKE TSALA-APOPKA LOOKING NORTH FROM THE FILL FLORAL CITY-FLA.

The above image was captured in the early 1940s from the shore near the Duval Island Bridge facing north into Lake Tsala Apopka, now the site of the public boat ramp. Duval Island is on the right, and the mainland is on the left. The image below, from the same time period, was taken from Duval Island looking west across the lake towards Floral City. Tsala Apopka, meaning "bass-eating place," is just one of many regional names coming from the Seminole (Muskogee) language. Others include Withlacoochee, "Little Big Black River"; Chassahowitzka, "Hanging Pumpkins"; Homosassa, "Wild Pepper Place"; Istachatta, "Red Men"; Weekiwachee, "Little Spring" or "Winding River"; Holathlikaha, "Shining"; E-Nini-Hassee, "Her Sunny Road"; and Panasoffkee, "Deep Valley of Lakes." The Muskogee name for Crystal River was Weewahi Iaca, or "Clear Water." Some of these names are difficult to pronounce, but they flow easily from the tongues of locals.

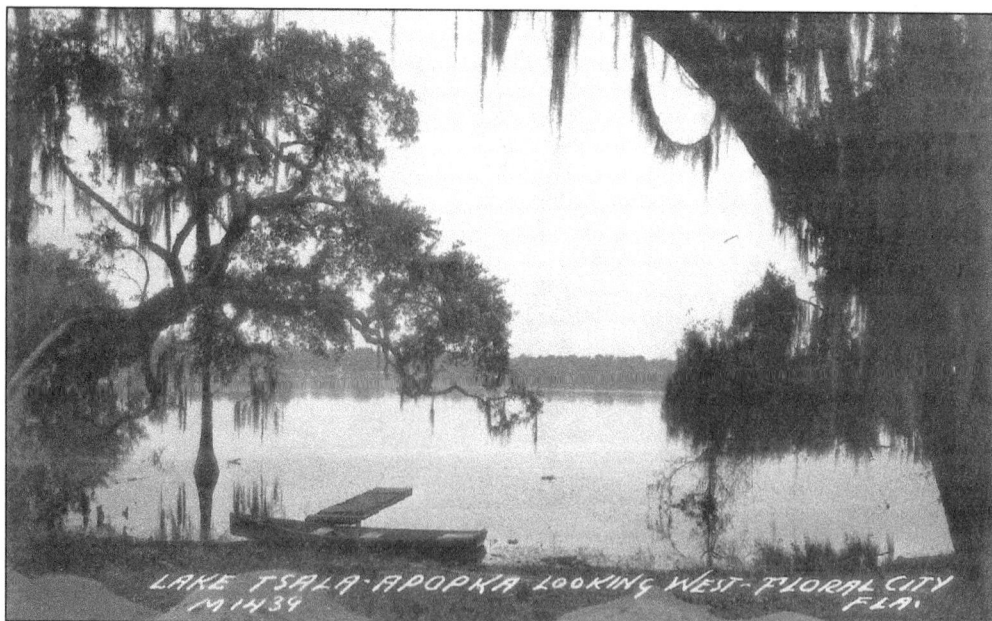

LAKE TSALA-APOPKA LOOKING WEST-FLORAL CITY FLA.

Seven

THE TOWNSPEOPLE

The New Hope Methodist Church cemetery, located on Istachatta Road (Route 39), was established in the mid-19th century and contains the remains of many regional pioneers. One noteworthy grave is that of Francis Townsend (1838–1912), shown in the foreground. He served as a US soldier in the Third Seminole War, a Confederate soldier in the Civil War, county tax collector, and later a state representative from Hernando County, which included what would later become Citrus County.

The serene Hills of Rest Cemetery along Route 41, just north of downtown Floral City, was established in 1884, one year after the town was founded. By 1952, however, it was nearly filled, so more adjacent land was purchased from Doc Ferris, owner of Ferris Groves in Floral City. Ferris died in 1975 and is buried in this cemetery, along with his wife, Harriet.

Two small historic African American cemeteries are located along Great Oaks Drive. They both are on the Florida Black History Trail. The Frasier Cemetery, shown here, began in 1908 as a private family burial site and contains numerous unnamed graves from the phosphate period. In 1966, it became officially known as the Floral City Community Cemetery. Just south of it is the tiny Williams Cemetery with about a dozen headstones.

Between 1889 and 1891, seven elections were held to determine the permanent government seat of newly formed Citrus County. Floral City, Mannfield, Lecanto, and Inverness were the towns in the running. The seventh vote barely decided in favor of Inverness over Mannfield, which had been the interim government seat. The results were contested, but before the Mannfield proponents could enact an injunction, Sheriff Priest implemented the movement of all county records and equipment to Inverness. Clerk of the court W.C. Zimmerman (right), a Floral City resident, refused to vacate his Mannfield office, so the movers physically lifted him up onto the wagon and transported him to Inverness still seated in his chair, at his desk, performing official business. In 1926, when Zimmermann was quite elderly, his brother Eugene (below with his horse) moved to Floral City to live with him.

Elisha Arnold Zellner was a Confederate veteran who lost his right arm during the war. He moved from Georgia to Florida with his family after the war and eventually settled in Cove Bend, a few miles east of Floral City, in the 1870s. Zellner established a cattle ranch, and he and his wife still have many descendants in the area.

Elisha Arnold Zellner

Hampton Dunn, standing in front of the family home, was a native of Floral City who distinguished himself both as a reporter for NBC and later as the managing editor of the *Tampa Daily News*. He is a well-published author of Florida history and is locally famous as the preeminent historian of Citrus County. His book *Back Home, a History of Citrus County, Florida* is required reading for area history buffs.

These were some of the prominent Floral City businessmen at the turn of the 20th century. Frank Baker (left), was the brother of original land owner Jim Baker. W.H. Havron (center) was a surveyor who platted the town (with state senator Austin Mann) as well as a lawyer and realtor. Wesley Duval (right) was John Paul Formy-Duval's son who was a citrus grower on Duval Island and a land developer.

Celeste E. "Nettie" (Formy-Duval, left) Baker, wife of Jim Baker; her sister Alverda (Formy-Duval) Baker, wife of Frank Baker, and their sister-in-law Annie (Baker) Havron, wife of W.H. Havron, pose for an outdoor photograph with Lota Hudson.

Here am I at Fifty-five,
With Preacher Perkins by my side;
He's trying so hard to save my hide,
But I'm taking time out to send Yuletide
Greetings from the sticks,
For you and yours in Fifty-six.
"Doc" Ferris

Doc Ferris was highly successful in his agricultural venture, producing award-winning citrus fruit that was shipped all over America and even to a few foreign countries. He constantly promoted his fruit as well as Citrus County and Floral City. It seemed to be second nature to him, and his outgoing personality made him locally famous and frequently in the news. He was also often seen with celebrities.

Doc Ferris, ever the showman, often produced entertaining and amusing Christmas cards to send to his friends and clients. This one says, "Here I am at Fifty-five, / With Preacher Perkins by my side; / He's trying so hard to save my hide, / But I'm taking time out to send Yuletide. / Greeting from the sticks, / For you and yours in Fifty-six. / 'Doc' Ferris."

Friends pose with Edward and Maude St. John on their wedding day. They stand in front of the St. John's home, Shadowbright, near the shore of Lake Consuela. The party includes, from left to right, Hazel Flood, Edward St. John, H.D. Bassett Jr., Maude St. John, Flossie Bassett, a Mrs. Tooke, and the unidentified minister and his wife who had just married them. The unique Floral City house below was constructed with limestone rocks in the 1930s according to St. John's design. St. John, a botanist, traveled the world studying and collecting plants. He had established beautiful *Billbergia* bromeliads on the property, and when he died in 1953, Maude placed similar bromeliads on all the live oak trees along Orange Avenue. These memorial plants are no longer there, but many specimens of this bromeliad still grow in the area.

Young Nick Metz enjoys playing cowboy with a dead alligator about 1930. The 1927 Ford Model T automobile behind him belonged to his namesake, his uncle Nick Metz. Before 1962, alligators were hunted extensively by locals for their valuable leather, as a source of meat, and occasionally simply to rid an area of large carnivores. In addition, many winter visitors enjoyed hunting alligators for sport. In 1962, alligators were given complete state protection, which lasted until 1988, when the state of Florida began sanctioning annual licensed harvests.

116

Eight

MODERN TIMES

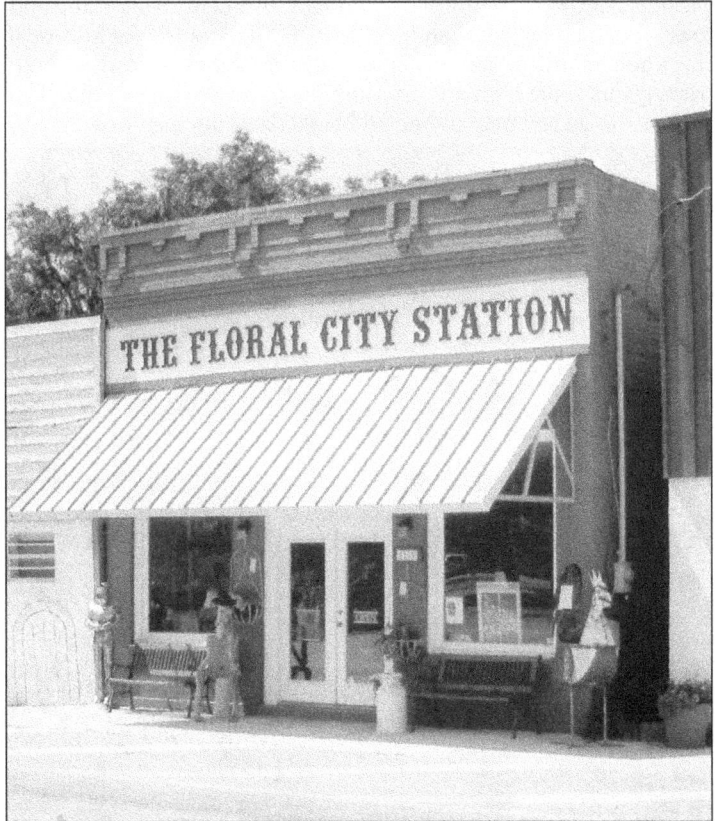

The handsome Floral City station, which still stands at the northeast corner of the main intersection, was built around 1900. It was the only brick building constructed in the downtown area at the time. Although it originally housed the Bank of Floral City, the bank closed when the mining industry folded. The building became the post office for a few years before being occupied by a succession of retail shops.

Since 1993, Floral City Heritage Days has occurred on the first Saturday in December. This affair is put on by the Floral City Heritage Council, a subsidiary of the Citrus County Historical Society. Members of the community dress in late-19th-century clothing and re-create the ambiance the town possessed in those long-ago days. While it promotes historical education, it is also fun for the whole family. Many owners of historic homes open their houses to the public, and other participants come from all over the state to set up displays of folkloric and historical traditions, such as the sugarcane grinding and basket-making seen here.

One of the most popular demonstrations at the annual Floral City Heritage Days celebration is the cracker cow hunter's camp (above), providing an authentic look at what life was like in this part of Florida during the annual cattle drives. Another popular display, sponsored by the Citrus Model A Club, displays antique automobiles. This annual celebration has become an important part of the Floral City community.

Many of the historic buildings scattered around Floral City have been lost in the past few decades. Some were lost to neglect and others have suffered fire or storm damage. Nevertheless, many Floral City historic structures have been saved, and several of these have been converted into successful businesses, including the Frugal Frog in the 1925 Bellot House (above) and Forgotten Treasures in the 1930 Harrison House (below).

Floral City's railway depot was deactivated shortly before World War II and was torn down in the early 1950s, but the railway still saw some use up to the mid-1980s. The Atlantic Coast Line railway, which ran through Floral City, was taken over by the Sea Board Coast Line in 1967, and then by CSX Transportation in 1980. Railroad traffic had already diminished considerably by the time this 1982 photograph was taken.

The railway was phased out of operation in the mid-1980s, and the tracks were taken up in 1987. Fortunately, the railway easement was incorporated into the Florida Rails-to-Trails network and is now the Withlacoochee State Trail, administered by the Florida Department of Parks and Recreation. Floral City is located exactly at the halfway point of this scenic, paved, 46-mile bicycle, hiking, and equestrian trail.

Floral City Heritage Council members constructed this gazebo on the Withlacoochee State Trail in 1997. Funded by the Emma Love Jenrette Memorial Fund, it was donated to the state park for use as a bicyclist and equestrian rest stop as well as a central meeting point for the townspeople. The gazebo is located at the site of the old Floral City train depot, near the crossing at Orange Avenue.

Today, in addition to citrus, Ferris Farms has become a major producer of commercial strawberries. As a result, Floral City hosts a strawberry festival every March. The farm also raises cattle and produces its own hay for feed, as shown in this foggy morning image. This farming activity on the outskirts of Floral City helps maintain the rural nature of the community so important to residents.

Both of these images celebrate the Floral City's history and help beautify the town. The above painting, *Floral City Heritage Days*, is by Floral City resident Mildred Polly Bernard, who unveiled it to the community on October 26, 2004. An accomplished folk artist who has been painting since the late 1940s, Bernard has exhibited her work in the Grandma Moses Exhibition of Primitive Art at the Orlando Museum of Arts. Below is the magnificent 50-foot-long mural depicting the town center, painted by Ann Covington on the east wall of Floral City Hardware. Covington established the Florida Artists Gallery in 2012.

The commercial center today is smaller than in past periods and has changed considerably through the years. Many of the original buildings in the downtown district were destroyed by fires in the early and mid-1900s. Since then, the commercial center has changed very little in appearance, although many businesses have come and gone and shifted around among the various historic buildings.

This is the official town center, not to be confused with the commercial center located just to the west, near Route 41. The town center includes four buildings and a landscaped frontage along Orange Avenue consisting of, from left to right, the Heritage Hall museum and country store, the Community House, the new Floral City Library, and the Masonic Lodge, barely visible on the far right.

124

Surprisingly, local people have received environmental benefits from the abandoned phosphate pits. Several of the flooded pits now provide steep-sided lakes for water-oriented recreation, and others, such as the Holder Mine in the Withlacoochee State Forest, shown here, have become heavily forested and include beautiful, lush, photogenic fern grottos that provide good wildlife habitats.

One modern change to the agriculture of Floral City is the replacement of extensive citrus groves with slash pine forestry. Introduced citrus trees are not immune to damage or destruction from hard freezes, but native pines are completely resistant to the cold. The pine trees once so important to the turpentine and lumber industries have now returned in abundance as managed agriculture.

Both historians and archaeologists still have plenty to keep them busy around Floral City. For instance, these carefully arranged limestone boulders on an island in Lake Tsala Apopka are very curious. Some say they are remains of slave houses, while others think they are old animal enclosures.

Archaeologist Rich Estabrook (left) and Dave Noble, past chairman of the Floral City Heritage Council, use a ground-penetrating radar machine to search for the unmarked graves of pioneer John Paul Formy-Duval and his family. Historical research indicates this site was the Duval family cemetery, but the headstones were lost long ago. The survey revealed several probable side-by-side graves, which will be marked with a memorial stone.

Soon after Fire Station No. 1 was closed in 2002, the Floral City Heritage Council was given permission by the Citrus County Commission to use the building as a display hall. Residents immediately set to work renovating, patching, and painting the building and had it ready as a museum in time for the annual Heritage Days celebration of 2004. After that success, the county gave the Heritage Council permission to use it as the official town museum. Many residents have donated historical objects and artifacts to help people, especially schoolchildren, learn and appreciate how people lived long ago right here in Floral City. The museum periodically changes the featured subjects in the main display room to diversify the educational aspects of its exhibits.

www.ingramcontent.com/pod-product-compliance
Lightning Source LLC
Chambersburg PA
CBHW080632110426
42813CB00006B/1662